Robert's Guide to Commercial Real Estate Investments

Insider Secrets to Commercial Real Estate Investing

By Robert A. Morse

Outskirts Press, Inc.
Denver, Colorado

Robert's Guide to Commercial Real Estate Investments
Insider Secrets to Commercial Real Estate Investing
All Rights Reserved.
Copyright © 2008 Robert A. Morse
V1.0

Outskirts Press, Inc.
http://www.outskirtspress.com

ISBN: 978-1-4327-1931-9

Outskirts Press and the "OP" logo are trademarks belonging to Outskirts Press, Inc.

PRINTED IN THE UNITED STATES OF AMERICA

Dedicated to my parents for their
wisdom, values, and integrity

Table of Contents

Introduction

Over the years I have searched for books on commercial real estate investing. I have discovered there are very few up-to-date books with much substantial content focused on the investor. This is a big business with lots of players but still very little information on this business seems to get published:

The intent of this book is to fill a gap in Commercial Real Estate books and to give you the basics of investing from an insider's point of view. It will include both **technical** AND **practical** information on commercial real estate investing. This business is not exceptionally difficult to understand, but it does take a lot of work to succeed.

This book will take an honest and straightforward approach. My intention is to give honest viewpoints and opinions that should provide a baseline to start from. I am writing it in the hopes that it will provide some information and dispel some common myths. This can save a lot of mistakes and wasted time at the beginning of any commercial real estate investment endeavor and help in the long-term with making money in commercial real estate investments.

Please bear with me on the more technical parts of this book, like the sections on "the numbers" and financing. These sections will be more difficult to read and take more time to understand. However, any analysis of a property will need to include a financial investigation. This will take some time, some effort, and, yes, some math.

Understanding the numbers is crucial to analyzing a property. If you are completely uncomfortable with math then you may want to consider a different career path. Commercial real estate may not be your calling. In this book I will include just enough information to give a fundamental understanding while using only basic math. In other words, I will keep it as simple as I can.

This is not a sales techniques book and this is not a "rah-rah" motivational book. There are already a huge number of outstanding sales and motivational books written. It is probably a good idea to find ones that fit your own style and personality. These are ones most likely to help.

Regrettably, we live in a very litigious world and I need to include the following: I am neither an attorney nor an accountant. I am not a broker in all states. Income taxes will not be treated in this book. It is simply just too broad of a subject to include here. You and your tax and legal advisors should always conduct your own investigation of any property and any transaction. All information in this book is from sources believed to be reliable. However, its accuracy cannot be guaranteed for all situations and we make no guarantee, warranty or representation about it. It is submitted subject to the possibility of errors, omissions, changes, or other conditions. Any projections, opinions, assumptions or estimates are for example only, and they may not represent current or future performance of a property.

I have attempted to write this book so each chapter can stand on its own; however there are some concepts that are closely intertwined and cannot be easily separated. I will make references between chapters as little as possible to make this book more readable and useful.

Good Luck, Good Reading, and Good Investing

Robert A. Morse

www.TheLoanLine.com

Chapter 1 - The Basic Food Groups:
Industrial, Office, Retail, and Multifamily

There are 4 main types of commercial properties: **Industrial**, **Office**, **Retail**, and **Multifamily**. In addition, there are **Special Purpose** properties. All of these are typically purchased to generate income from rents and so are often called **Income Properties**. The names of these types of properties are, for the most part, self-explanatory, but this chapter has some important additional details to understand.

- Industrial
- Office
- Retail
- Multifamily
- Special Purpose

Industrial

Industrial space is just as one would guess. It is used for functions like warehousing, manufacturing, printing, distribution, and other industrial uses. As a "rule of thumb", Industrial space is typically the least expensive per square foot to purchase or lease.

There are different levels of industrial usage. Many people call it **Light Industrial** or **Heavy Industrial** for lighter and heavier uses. However, this simple description over-generalizes and leaves out too much essential information. The only concrete way to understand what types of uses are allowed is to look at the **Zoning**[1] regulations set by the local government for that specific property.

Sometimes there are additional limitations imposed by the leases or by an owners' association. It is crucial to consider what types of uses are allowed at a given property. Some uses that may or may not be allowable are: outdoor storage, chemical and flammable storage, automotive storage, religious facilities. This will directly affect the type of tenants that an investor will be leasing to now and in the future.

Looking at current tenants and other nearby facilities is a good starting point to understand what is allowed, but remember that is just a "first-cut" investigation. The actual zoning will be very specific and more accurate.

A few important criteria for Industrial Space to consider are:

- What kind of manufacturing is allowed?

---

[1] Zoning is the set of rules that specify specific standards for building and allowed usage in a given location. These rules are typically set by local government, like a city following their general plan. See also the section on zoning.

- What kind of storage is allowed?
- Is there adequate power supply, water supply, sewer and drainage?
- What is the **Inside Height** of the space? Higher allows for more inside storage. This may be leased by cubic foot instead of square foot for warehouse type spaces.
- Are **Loading Docks**; **Dock High**[1], **Grade Level**, or not available?
- Is the property truck and or rail/train accessible?

Built Out Industrial Space

True industrial space is typically unfinished with no walls dividing it. This is commonly referred to as **Shell Condition**. However it is also common to have some part of an industrial space **Built Out** with walls for the offices that run the business. It is common to hear that a building is "20% Built-Out" which means that 20% of the square footage has been upgraded and finished to office space.

Industrial Office

In some areas where real estate values are very high and/or office space is in short supply it has become common practice to "build-out" the entire inside of industrial buildings as office space. These spaces are often used by "high-tech" companies that can operate in an industrial or business park setting. Although, these are not the only kind of company

---

[1] Dock high loading docks are at the height of the truck that backs up to them so that the inside of the truck is level with the floor so forklifts can easily unload a truck, while grade level docks are at the same level as the ground outside where trucks drive up.

operating this way. Remember, always refer to the zoning, leases, and owners' association for the allowed uses.

Office

Office commercial real estate is just as the name implies; it is office space. This is space typically used for white collar workers like:

- Attorneys
- Accountants
- Engineering Firms
- Commercial real estate brokers and mortgage brokers
- And others who primarily work on a computer or on paper in an information-driven environment.

As a "rule of thumb" office space is typically the more expensive to purchase or lease per square foot than industrial space because it often:

- Has more features built into the building for the tenants (often called **Tenant Improvements** or **TI's**.
- Requires more parking than industrial space[1]
- Offers more services from the management company.

However, many people can move into an office space with minimal changes to the building which can make leasing space easier, faster, and less costly for both the tenant and property owner.

---

[1] Office space typically has more employees per square foot than industrial space and so needs more land for parking which adds cost to the building.

Medical Office Space

Medical Office Space is also normally considered office space, but it has the distinction of being filled with doctors, dentists, veterinarians, etc. It has some significant differences from regular office space. It usually requires considerable improvements to a building for the specific use (commonly known as tenant improvements).

Doctors, dentists, and veterinarians tend to have lots of specific plumbing and electrical requirements that can be very expensive to install and/or change. Another big issue for medical office space is that there are additional parking requirements to handle the extra patient parking in addition to the regular employees. These extra requirements typically mean the rents are higher for a medical building because there is more building customization (or TI's) and extra land required for parking.

Retail

Retail space is just as the name implies. It is space for retail storefronts. This is where people go to purchase products and services. This includes retailers like large drugstore chains, grocery stores, electronics retailers, clothing stores, jewelry stores, dry-cleaners and any store that is selling a product or service to the public. This includes the giant **Big Box** stores like the large drugstore chains, home improvement stores, and supermarkets; and everything all the way down to the small **Mom-and-Pop Stores**[1] in a strip mall.

Parking and easy access are two principal considerations for any retail building.

- If there's not enough parking, customers will look for more convenient shopping.
- If it is difficult to get into and out of a retail center, customers will look for more convenient shopping.

Poor parking means fewer sales for tenants, lower income for tenants, and the potential for higher vacancies in the retail building. Do not underestimate the value of adequate parking and easy access to a retail building. Shoppers want convenience and will look elsewhere if they don't get it.

It is interesting to note that sometimes churches, schools, and daycare will be located in retail centers. Zoning often allows for this type of use. These uses often require a plenty of parking spaces that retail space typically has. And many times they are used in "off hours" for the retail center so it does not impact the other tenants in the center.

Single Purpose Retail Space

Fast food places, other restaurants, and some retailers often have a building that's built specifically for them. These tenants can be great tenants, but be sure they have a good lease guaranteed by solid company and/or a financially strong individual. This is

---

[1] Small locally owned businesses are often referred to as "Mom and Pop" which is an older reference to a family owned and run business.

to ensure the rent is paid no matter what happens. These are usually very customized buildings with lots of TI's. If for some reason the tenant defaults on their lease and stops paying, it can be difficult to lease it to someone else.   This could result in a prolonged vacancy and/or accepting a lower rental rate in the future or expensive remodeling.

Multifamily (5 Units and More)

Multifamily (5+ Units) is a "different animal" altogether. Many people think of it as **Commercial Residential**. In some ways it can be thought of as a cross between commercial and residential real estate. Multifamily properties are just another name for apartment buildings. These properties typically have much weaker "residential" leases than the commercial properties already discussed above.

There are many residential property laws and common practices that apply only to properties that have up to four units. Multifamily properties with 5 or more units are typically considered "commercial" real estate because the laws and common practices change significantly at 5 units.   This book is not addressing residential real estate, so it will cover only "Commercial Multifamily" properties with 5 or more units.

The financing, insurance, laws, and common practices for "commercial" Multifamily are significantly different from residential real estate. Someone who is more familiar with true **Residential (1-4 units)** properties should be sure to understand the differences before making any commitments.

An important source of additional income may come from laundry rooms, parking spots, garages, and extra storage.

The amenities (like pools, jacuzzi's, tennis courts, etc.) at a multifamily property tend to draw tenants and higher rents, but also usually incur more expenses for maintenance.   It is important to investigate this tradeoff before investing.

Mobile Home Parks

Mobile Home Parks can be considered a part of Multifamily real estate or as a completely separate property type. They have some similarities and some striking differences.   Mobile Home Parks provide **Pads/Spaces** for the mobile homes, roads, electrical hook-ups, plumbing hook-ups, and various amenities. These properties operate very differently from the other property types but are closest to Multifamily. The park may own some, none, or all of the mobile homes in the park. They rent out spaces and if they own mobile homes they can rent those out also. Additionally, there is potential for other income in buying and selling mobile homes as residents move out and move in.   Like multifamily, laundry income can be significant.

Special Purpose Properties

Special purpose properties are just as the name implies; properties built for a specific purpose. Above is mentioned one type of special purpose property, "Single Purpose Retail Space". However, there are many other types of special purpose property types such as:

- Schools
- Religious Facilities
- Golf Courses
- Marinas
- Hotels
- Self Storage Properties
- Night Clubs / Bars
- Truck Stops
- Gas Stations / Car Washes
- And many others

Financing and insurance can be a little more difficult to find for these properties. Many lending and insurance companies do not work with businesses like these, because they do not fit their **Risk Profile**. This essentially means that they do not fit their business model; or they do not know how to deal with these types of properties. These special purpose properties also usually need an investor and business operator that have experience in that business. With these additional risks an owner can also make a better return if he or she knows what they are doing. It is the standard **Risk vs. Return Tradeoff**; more risk usually means the potential for better returns.

Commercial is NOT Residential Real Estate

There are many differences between commercial and residential real estate. Financing, insurance, contracts, legal disclosures, escrow, and many other practices are different. Here are a few of the many differences.

- "Commercial" financing and insurance are required.

- There are different sales contracts for multifamily properties. Reading a standard multifamily sale contract is a great way to start to get familiar with some key differences.
- There are usually fewer specific legal disclosure "forms" required, but anything that should be reasonably known about the property must still be disclosed in a sale. This is less structured and more "open ended".
- A commercial escrow company needs to be used.
- Commercial financing, insurance, escrow, etc. tends to be more costly than residential.
- Terminology, financing requirements, and forms are usually very different.

This list could go on and on. The bottom line is: Commercial properties are handled very differently from residential properties. Be sure to understand the differences and be sure the brokers, attorneys, and accountants involved understand the differences. Use commercial real estate specialists whenever possible.

Chapter 2 - Introduction to Contracts:
Put It in Writing

Contracts are a way to document what everyone is agreeing to in a transaction. In commercial real estate, a contract could be a **Purchase Agreement**, **Lease Agreement**, or **Financing Agreement**. A contract is a list of everyone's duties and responsibilities or in other words their **Contractual Obligations**. It reduces confusion because it identifies and documents who is responsible for what.

When all the involved parties review a contract before signing it, it gives them a chance to look for potential problems in the contract. Then the contract can be revised so everyone can agree on responsibilities. This review and revision process is crucial to avoid disagreements in the future. Getting many people reviewing the contract also helps reduce the chance that something will be missed or overlooked.

As expected, everyone has to agree on these modifications by signing the final version of the revised contract. One party cannot unilaterally change a contract unless everyone agrees to it by signing off on the changes.

Only If It Is in the Contract

No matter what anybody promises, it only counts if it is agreed to in the contract. I'm not an attorney and there are probably legal exceptions to this rule, but I would not count on anything verbal or unsigned. For real estate if it is not written down and agreed to by all parties then do not rely on it at all.

When there are only verbal agreementsit is very easy for people to think they are agreeing, when in reality they are agreeing to different things. It may appear that there is an agreement when there is not. It is easy for misunderstandings to occur. Additionally, over time peoples' memory of what they "agreed to" may get clouded and ambiguous. This is where legal problems are likely to start. Why risk it? Put it in a signed contract just to be safe.

Additionally, there are some unscrupulous people out there who will lie. If it is in a contract this makes it more difficult for them to lie and much easier to get caught in a lie. Now, contracts do not automatically protect you from dishonest people, but they document agreements and give you recourse if somebody does not follow through on their promise. There is an expression that "locks keep honest people honest". Well, contracts can be thought of the same way but they can also be used to punish the dishonest.

If it is not in the contract then do not rely on it!

Contracts – A Way to Avoid Lawsuits?

A well written contract should never have to be used in a lawsuit. It should be so clear and so well written that each of the parties involved understands completely what is expected of them and what they expect from the other parties. Lawsuits can happen when someone doesn't understand the contract, the contract is vague, or someone just is not living up to their end of the agreement. Not many people want to be part of a lawsuit, so I recommend making contracts as clear as possible to reduce the chance of a lawsuit.

Understand Before Signing Anything

Always understand any contracts you plan to sign, before you sign them! Always, understand the terms and legal definitions. And most importantly understand the implications of the contract. If you don't understand something then get advice from your broker, legal counsel, and/or tax advisor.

Real estate contracts can seem overwhelming at first. To be honest, they can be downright boring. However, it is vital, especially when starting out, to read through them, even if it is difficult. With practice and experience it gets easier to scan contracts because much of the content is very similar in many contracts. Always be careful to not scan too quickly or something important could be missed. As a rule of thumb, scan each paragraph in a contract at least enough so its purpose is clear. Otherwise it is too easy to miss something important. And make sure an extra paragraph did not get added somewhere.

One other rule of thumb is very helpful: Pay close attention to the first few pages AND the last few pages of the contract. The first few pages are obvious because these pages usually set the basic terms for the agreement. Then the contract goes into more detail.

However, it is much less obvious to read the last few pages carefully also. This is where fine tuning and additional terms of the contract are often added. Many mistakes and crucial details can be caught here. **The entire contract is important, but many mistakes can be avoided by carefully reading the beginning AND end of the contract**.

Executed Contracts

Contracts are meaningless until they become **Executed**. Executed just means: signed by all the parties agreeing to the contract. So the term executed, simply means agreed to and signed. Another term you may hear is, **Counterpart** or **Signed-In-Counterpart**. This simply means that different parties signed different copies of the same document. For most cases this is completely acceptable and the same as if signed on the same copy. There is one caveat; the different copies must be EXACTLY the same. Otherwise there would be different people agreeing to different contractual obligations which could lead to confusion, disagreements, and lawsuits. There could even be the question of whether there was any agreement at all. If a contract is signed in counterpart be sure the copies are all exactly the same.

Leasing and Investments

Does someone investing and only making purchases need to understand leasing contracts? ABSOLUTELY! Do not overlook this! **Investors need to understand lease contracts (leases).** The income from investment real estate comes from leases. When an investor buys a property he is expecting income from the current and future tenants. The amount of income and many of the investor's expenses will be determined by the leases already in place and what kind of lease terms can be expected in the future as new tenants move-in.

Chapter 3 - Commercial Real Estate Terms:
Understand the Language

The first step to learning anything, including Commercial Real Estate Investing is: Understand the language and terminology so it can be discussed intelligently. There are many common terms used and misused.

Understanding correct terminology and using it properly is crucial to project a professional image. Experienced investors, brokers, accountants, property managers, and attorneys are much more likely to take someone seriously if they have a polished and professional image.

The discussion of the types of Commercial Real Estate in the earlier chapter is the starting point to learn the vocabulary of this business. However, there are many more. This chapter will introduce more general language; and then even more terms will be introduced throughout this book.

Real Estate and Improvements

Real estate is the land and all improvements that are affixed to the land. **Improvements** are anything added and **Permanently Attached** or **Affixed** to the land that "improves it". This includes buildings, landscaping, fences, walls, wells, etc. Most things are easy to determine if they are an "affixed" part of the property or not. The building is permanently attached to the land and on a foundation and so is part of the real estate. However, a tractor on the property is clearly not part of the real estate because it is easily moved and not attached to the property.

When a business is involved, there may be equipment that is part of the real estate. This is tricky and it is probably best to involve a **Business Broker**[1] or clearly specify in any contracts what is part of the real estate and what is not. This removes any room for misunderstandings caused by interpretations. If in doubt, write it down in the contract before signing.

Leasing & Purchasing

Leasing simply means; renting under certain agreed-on conditions that are specified in the lease contract. The **Lease Contract** is simply a list that documents everyone's responsibilities and expectations. **Purchasing** or Investing means (yes, you guessed it) buying a property as an investment.

Investors need to understand both leasing and investing terms, not just investing terms. Why? The

---

[1] A broker who buys and sells businesses – Remember a business sale often does not include the real estate. It is the sale of a business that may or may not include real estate.

income from investment real estate comes from leases. When an investor buys a property he or she is expecting income from the current and future tenants. The amount of income and many of the investor's expenses will be determined by the leases already in place and what kind of lease terms can be expected in the future as new tenants move-in.

Owner-User

The term **Owner-User** is a commonly used term in the commercial real estate business. If someone is buying a property to move into it themselves, for their own business, this is called an "owner-user". Generally this type of purchase is primarily for a business purpose and only secondarily as an investment, so this is not really an investment property. It is not purchased to generate rent; it is purchased to run a business.

Parcel Number or Assessor's Parcel Number (APN)

A basic principle of all real estate is that each piece of property is unique. The property next door or across the street may be similar, but it is never exactly the same. Properties can be identified uniquely by their Parcel Number or Assessor's Parcel Number (APN). This is the tax assessor's number to identify the property for tax purposes. Each parcel or property will have its own unique identifying number. This is important to know so that a property can be properly and uniquely identified when researching it as a potential investment.

Notice that some sales will include multiple parcels and so will have multiple numbers. Be sure to know when this is the case so that all of the property in the sale is investigated.

Zoning

Zoning is the set of rules that set **specific** standards for construction and allowed uses in a given location. It is a way to control land usage and construction to control congestion and conflicting property uses and rights. Zoning rules are usually set by the local government, like a city or county. Typically, cities create a **General Plan** to guide how they grow. This general plan sets the zoning laws so the city grows with some control on **Development** and **Redevelopment**[1].

Without any zoning there could be a single family residence, an automotive repair shop, a bar, a recycling plant, and a 30 story high rise office building right next to each other. Without zoning it is likely that there would be congestion, conflicts between property owners, and many other problems caused by haphazard development.

Zoning rules specify the type of allowed uses (residential, industrial, office, retail, and multifamily. Common rules set in zoning laws are:

- Allowed Business Types, for example heavy manufacturing, doctors offices, or retail shopping centers

---

[1] Redevelopment is when buildings are torn down and rebuilt or significantly modified.

- Setbacks – how close to a property line can a building be built
- Building Height
- Parking Requirements – number of spaces, size of parking spaces, required access including width of driving areas
- **Parking Ratio** – typically expressed as a the minimum number of parking spots required per 1,000 square feet of building space, for example 5 per 1000 is a common requirement for medical office space, while 4 per 1000 is a common requirement for general office space and usually less for typical industrial space.

Zoning is a very complex subject. The list above is a very small subset of possible zoning regulations. The only true way to understand specific zoning requirements is to look at the zoning code itself because it varies from city to city. Fortunately, many cities and counties have this information online for free; **if** you can find it. Search online for "zoning" or "planning" on your city or county website. The hardest part is finding the right part of code that applies. Once you find it be sure to remember where it is located in the regulations.

It may seem a bit "mind numbing" to look at the city zoning laws at first, but it gets much easier with just a little practice. To find zoning information for a specific property, first find the **Zoning Designation** for a property from tax records or a title company and then look up the zoning regulations for that area. A zoning designation is a few letters and/or numbers used to easily identify the type of zoning in the zoning laws. It is just a notation to make it easier to refer to the type of zoning. For example, zoning designations may look like:

- R1 for single family residential
- R2, R3, R4 for multifamily with increasing densities of units
- M1, M2, M3, I1,I2, I3 for industrial uses
- O for office uses

Of course, each city has their own designations, but you are likely to see some similar to those shown above as examples.

Larger cities have considerably more complicated zoning laws, so expect to see many more zoning designations and many fine points in their zoning codes. Also, they can be very specific for certain areas because they may have **Redevelopment Districts**[1], areas with parking regulations, or areas with specific changes the city is trying to effect through zoning. There may be **Zoning Overlays**" where you will have the baseline zoning plus additional requirements specified in one or more "overlays". It can get very complicated. Many developers get very good at understanding zoning and how to develop the most building possible and still stay within the zoning regulations.

CUP or Conditional Use Permit

Some types of businesses are allowed in the zoning regulations, but require a special permit called a **CUP** or **Conditional Use Permit**. This is usually for

---

[1] Areas that the city wants redeveloped so the zoning incentivizes owners and developers to redevelop, often by allowing them to put in a larger building or giving some other benefit to the owner

a business that puts some sort of extra burden on the neighborhood like a church, a preschool, a private high school, or a bar that will add to traffic, parking congestion, and potential conflicts. This gives the local government a way to review and limit uses if the impact is too much for an area.

Class A, B, C

Class A, **Class B**, and **Class C** are terms that are often used very loosely. If 10 different people were asked for precise definitions for these terms, it is likely they would all be different.

Here are some guidelines to help sort through this:

- – Class A is the best quality
- – Class B is middle quality
- – Class C is lesser quality

Class A means the best quality building and/or neighborhood. This is often a building with full services. Many would define Class A as a prestigious building where image conscious tenants like advertising agencies, high-end attorneys, and high-end accountancy firms would be located. Class A office space is commonly used in major downtown areas and this seems to be one case where Class A has more meaning. Some people use Class A very freely; they call any of the "nicer" properties in an area "Class A". However, there are many others that might not call these same properties Class A. This is open to interpretation.

Most properties fall into the Class B category. They are neither pristine and prestigious nor are they on the lower end. They are in the "middle of the road". Since most properties could be described as class B, it makes these "class" designations less useful.

The Class C category is for run down buildings and/or worse neighborhoods.

Additionally, these "class" designations are often used for:

- the quality of the property overall, including the geographical area AND building
- the quality of the area only
- the quality of the building only

Someone may say, "I want a class C building in a Class B area". This means they want a lower quality building in a middle of the road area. Or they might simply mention Class A, B, or C in reference to a property. If they do not specify "building" or "area" they are usually referring to the property overall, including the building and area.

All of this is **very** subjective and open to interpretation. It is probably best for each investor to make their own determination of a property simply by looking at it and not relying on these designations too much. However, these are commonly used terms that are important to understand if they are heard.

Deferred Maintenance

Deferred Maintenance is work on the property that needs to be completed, but has not yet been done. It has been "deferred" to a later date. Deferred maintenance is not viewed favorably by buyers or lenders for a number of reasons.

One of the biggest reasons is that small problems like needing paint can quickly turn into large and **expensive** problems like water damage and dry rot. Or bad drainage can turn into foundation damage. Typically, it is much less expensive to keep up with maintenance than it is to "defer" it and eventually pay for the original required maintenance and subsequent damage. Things that need repair rarely get better on their own, but they often get much worse with neglect. How much does avoiding major car engine problems with regular oil changes cost as compared to a new engine in your car?

Many lenders will not even give financing if there is deferred maintenance above 2% - 5% of the property value. Insurance companies do not like it either and may not offer coverage because of it.

Tenants do not like deferred maintenance. Properties with deferred maintenance tend to look run-down and shabby. Often tenants that stay in properties with significant deferred maintenance are the ones paying below market rents or cannot get a lease anywhere else. These are not ideal tenants. As a result, deferred maintenance can cost an owner by having "less than ideal" tenants and consequently lost income.

Always consider the costs of lower income and higher expenses due to deferred maintenance in any property analysis. And remember financing and insurance can be problems if there is significant deferred maintenance.

Funded Reserves

Funded Reserves are money set aside or "reserved" every month for anticipated major repairs in the future. Since the money is saved in an account they are "funded". A few examples of likely major repairs are: roofs, air conditioners, and parking lot pavement. These things just wear out over time and use and eventually will need to be replaced.

There are many ways to calculate the amount set aside for reserves to assure enough is saved for future major repairs, but those details are beyond the scope of this book. The basic idea of reserves is to set aside enough money each month so that on average the reserve money will pay for future major repairs. In other words, take the expected cost to replace each major item in a property, like a roof, and then calculate how much needs to be set aside every month over the expected remaining life of each item to pay for the eventual replacement[1].

A reserve account is like a savings account for large expenses that an owner expects to have in the future. Reserves are not for the regular day-to-day maintenance items, like door repairs or replacing light bulbs. These would just be regular ongoing expenses.

Beware of Pro Forma

Pro Forma means what "could" be done for income and expenses on a property. It is just an estimate or a projection for the future. It is not current

---

[1] Including inflation and interest earned on money saved

actual income and expenses!   It is only what somebody believes COULD be achieved if ...   If what? This is one of those terms to understand and be very aware of what it means.

If it could be done, why hasn't it been done? Sometimes there are valid reasons that the current owner has not raised rents or reduced expenses. Good examples of this are if the owner has a relationship with a tenant and so does not want to raise the rent; or maybe the owner has a service provider (like a plumber or manager) he knows personally and so doesn't want to change to a lower cost provider.

Another common example is if the property needs some work and so rents are low and expenses are high. And the owner just does not want to deal with the hassle of fixing-up the property.   In this case maybe the property could be fixed-up, rents increased, and ongoing maintenance costs reduced. However, even in this case, why buy a property based on Pro Forma numbers when the new owner will have to do the work to improve the property. If the investor pays for an improved property they should get an improved property, not just the option to improve it. Most experienced investors do not take Pro Forma numbers very seriously.

Okay, those are all valid possibilities and there are others, but they are not the norm. It seems that most of the time Pro Forma means "Fantasy Land" for whoever "made-up" the Pro Forma projections. Remember these are estimates based on someone's judgment. Never base a property analysis only on Pro Forma income and expenses. Ask for the actual historical income and expense numbers for your analysis. These are often referred to as **Actuals**. The actuals are probably more relevant and usually give you a better picture of the property.

Tenants do not pay Pro Forma rents, owners do not pay Pro Forma expenses nor do they deposit Pro Forma earnings into their bank account. Do not base any analysis on Pro Forma values unless there is a valid reason. If it could be done, why hasn't the current owner done it yet?

Under Market

Under Market means that the price that is being charged is below what is generally being paid for a similar item in the market. This can apply to lease rates or the price of a property for sale.

Rents can be under market due to poor management. A manager or owner that is not raising rents to keep up with the market makes tenants happy, but loses potential income.

If rents are truly below the market value, it is a great opportunity to increase the income on the property by raising rents. This is when a Pro Forma analysis could be useful. But be very careful, market rents are difficult to determine.

A good "reality check" for rental rates is:

- If there are no vacancies then rents are probably too low
- If the vacancy rate is much higher than other nearby similar properties then the rents are probably too high.

A sale price can be under market for a large number of reasons. It is often related to rents being under market which means the building is not at its optimal earning potential. Sometimes it is under market because a seller does not understand the value of a building or they have to sell a property quickly because of other investment opportunities or financing problems.

Underperforming

Another common term used in this business is an **Underperforming Property** which simply means the property is not delivering (or performing) to its full potential because it has issues like management problems, vacancies, or deferred maintenance that have not been resolved.

If a property is truly under market or underperforming, it can be an opportunity for an investor to make money by fixing the problems, raising the rents, and bringing the property up to market value.

Chapter 4 - Leasing:
Crucial for Investors Also

Investors, not just tenants, need to understand lease contracts because income from an investment property is set by the leases. The most common reason an investor buys a property is for the income it generates from tenants, so the leases are crucial for any commercial real estate investment.

Lease Contracts[1]

A very simple explanation of a **Lease Contract** is: "a list of tenant responsibilities, limitations, and costs as well as a list of owner/landlord responsibilities, limitations, and payments to be received from the tenant". **Tenants** are the people or businesses renting space and the **Owner** is the **Landlord** who rents out the space. The tenant pays rent and often reimburses the owner for certain expenses specified

---

[1] Lease contracts are often just called leases

in the lease. In exchange the tenant gets the use of the space they are leasing.

Remember, any provisions that an owner and tenant want to include in a lease can be included; As long as they do not break any laws. So if it is important to the landlord or the tenant then it can probably be written-into the lease. Of course they have to reach agreement on these terms first.

There is no way to cover every potential alternative that could be incorporated into a lease contract. This section is an introduction to show the basics and allow an investor to start analyzing leases, not to explain every possible detail. Leasing contracts are a broad enough subject by themselves to write another entire book.

Lease Term

The **Lease Term** is the amount of time the tenant promises to rent the property from the landlord as specified in the lease contract. It is commonly 3, 5, 7, or more years for commercial properties[1]. However, it can be any length of time. Landlords typically like to have longer term leases so they do not have to search for new tenants as often and have a known income from rent for a longer period of time.

Lease Options

Options are an opportunity to do "something" by a specified date. After that date the option expires and has no value to anybody. If no date were

---

[1] except for multifamily properties which typically have 1, 6, or 12 month leases.

specified then the option could be used at any time in the future, which is usually not a very good idea for the landlord.

An option is typically only a benefit to the option holder who is normally the tenant. They execute the option only if it is advantageous to them. Otherwise they do nothing and the option "expires". If a tenant has an "option" it means they have the right to implement the option but they are not required to use it.

Lease Renewal Options

A **Lease Renewal Option** is an option (not a requirement) for the tenant to renew the lease for a specified amount of time and at a specified rent. A typical example is a 5yr lease with three options to extend the lease for 5 years at a time. Of course the amount of rental increases would also have to be specified. These often follow a fixed percentage, an index like CPI, or the lesser/greater of these two methods.

The time for the lease extension, rental amount, and all other lease terms should be included in a well written lease. Vague lease options are a likely source for disagreements and lawsuits, so the lease contract should be very clear on lease renewal options to help avoid lawsuits.

Lease Expansion and Relocation Options

Other common tenant lease options are:

- **Lease Expansion Option** - Option to expand into other available space or in other words, rent additional space

> – **Lease Relocation Option** - Option to relocate into another available space

All the terms need to be specified in detail in the lease.

Once in a while there will be an **Option To Purchase** a property at terms specified in the lease. Or sometimes there is a **First Right of Refusal** Option which means the tenant has the first opportunity to purchase the property before it is offered on the open market. These can cause difficulties for the owner when he goes to sell a building because it may allow the tenant to delay or interfere with the sales process. Usually, these are not recommended without a good reason.

Remember options typically only benefit the tenant who has the option. They do not have to execute the option unless there is a benefit to them.

Rental Rate

Rental Rates are is usually specified as a rate given in price per square foot ($/sf) to make comparisons simpler and more meaningful. This allows comparisons to be made between spaces of different sizes. The rent for a 6,000sf[1] space should be more than the rent for a similar 5,000sf space. However, if the two spaces are similar their rental rates per sf should be close to the same.

The rental rate per sf for a 30,000sf space is probably not the same as a 1,000sf space. These are not really similar. Typically, for smaller spaces the

---

[1] Square Feet is commonly abbreviated as sf or SF

rate or price per square foot is more. Larger spaces get a lower rate per square foot which is like an "economy of scale"[1].

Rent Escalations / Increases

Rent Escalations or Increases are commonly included in a lease contract also. Rent may be raised annually or any other period of time such as every other year, every 5 years, or only when an option to extend the lease is taken. These are all often called **Stepped Rent Increases**). Rent increases are often a fixed percentage rate increase or may follow an index such as the Consumer Price Index (CPI) or a fixed dollar amount.

Rental Rates in Different Regions

Different regions quote rental rates differently and it makes an enormous difference. Some quote in dollars per square ft per **month ($/sf/mo)** while others quote in dollars per square ft per **year ($/sf/yr)**. So $12/sf/yr is equivalent to $1/sf/mo. There have been conversations out there that go something like this: "Wow, $5/sf in that area. That's a great deal! Why so inexpensive?"

Unfortunately, there is a misunderstanding in this case. This person thinks it is $5/sf/yr but the rate is $5/sf/mo which is actually $60/sf/yr (12 months x $5/sf/mo). That's a big difference. Most of the time it is obvious, but be aware of the differences in common practices like this that vary from one region to another.

---

[1] An Economy of Scale is like when you buy a 10 pack of something at the store and so the price per item is lower or at a lower rate than if you bought just one.

Proration or Pro Rata Share

Prorating simply means allocating each tenant's fair share of some cost or expense to the tenant. It is also often called their **Pro Rata** share.

It is fairly easy to understand proration through a simple example. Let's say there is a building with 100,000sf in it. The tenant that leases 20,000sf is leasing 20% of the total building (20,000sf / 100,000sf = 20%) so they pay 20% of the cost. Or 20% of the cost is allocated to them.

Tenant Improvements

Tenant Improvements (TI's) are modifications made to properties to customize the building for a tenant. The more specialized the space the more it costs to "improve" it and the more difficult it will be to find an alternative tenant in case the current tenant leaves or defaults on the lease.

Many leases state that the tenant is responsible to pay for all tenant improvements when they move-in and responsible to put the space back to its original condition when they move-out. This TI expense can be substantial and ties the tenant to the property. They will want to stay to benefit from the TI's they paid for.

However, tenants can default on a lease before they put the property back to its original condition so the owner would have to pay to restore the space or try to lease it out "as is". However, if tenants are paying higher rents to compensate an owner for this risk then it is often a good tradeoff.

Tenant Improvements can be very expensive for tenants like doctors, dentists, and restaurants. However, doctors and dentists are often good tenants to have for a number of reasons. They tend to make a good income so they are likely to be able to pay their rent.   They have invested a lot of money in tenant improvements and so are tied to the space. And they are not likely to move because it might cause them to lose patients and referrals.   In summary, they are not likely to default on a lease and typically want long term leases and/or leases with lots of options to extend the lease. This is all very similar for a restaurant, except restaurants are usually much riskier.

As a rule of thumb, fewer tenant improvements are typically better because it takes less time to lease up a space that is fairly "generic" and many kinds of tenants could use it "as is". But there are exceptions like doctors and dentists.

Tenant Allowance

Landlords may "give" a new tenant a **Tenant Allowance**. This means the owner will pay up to the amount of the "tenant allowance" for improvements and the tenant will have to pay for improvements beyond that amount. It is usually quoted as a dollar amount per square foot leased ($/sf) or as a fixed amount for leasing a space.

The word "give" is in quotations above because the landlord often charges more for rent if there is a tenant allowance. The tenant, in effect, pays back the cost of the improvements over the term of the lease. This seems fair; the tenant is the one who will get the benefit of the improvements. In essence, they are renting a more improved and customized space so the rent should be higher.

Very often a tenant allowance will not cover much more than the most basic improvements so the tenant will have to pay for anything beyond just basic upgrades. Many landlords will allow the tenant to pay for tenant improvements over time with their rent payments. This is the same thing as increasing rent payments to pay for additional improvements. Again, this makes sense because the tenant is paying for the improvements they will get the benefit from. "Pay here" or "pay there"; not much is truly for free. It is usually just included in the price.

Market Rents and Rent Surveys

Market Rent is the price of rent that tenants are generally willing to pay for comparable properties in a given area. That's easy, Right? Not really.

Comparable Properties

First of all; What is "Comparable"? **Comparable** is what potential tenants consider to be very similar or almost interchangeable. Very few properties are very similar. They have different amenities & services, different accessibility, different public images, different sizes, and many, many other factors. The more similar two properties are the more comparable they are. Comparability is not black-and-white, instead is a scale from almost exactly the same to not the same at all. Remember, it is a comparison **relative to the building being evaluated**. The building under evaluation is typically called the **Subject Property**.

Comparability is a judgment call and is open to interpretation. Each evaluator must decide what is comparable and what is not and to what degree. Experienced investors usually get very good at judging what is comparable and how comparable it is.

Rent Surveys

Finding the market level rent is not a simple task. A **Rent Survey** seems to be the only reliable way to estimate market rents for a given property. It is a time-consuming but valuable task.

A "rent survey" is a survey of owners, property managers, online leasing databases, and lease listing brokers that work with comparable properties. This means calling as many owners, managers, and brokers as can be found with "similar[1]" properties and asking them what are their rental rates in dollars per square foot[2], reimbursed expenses, lease terms, **Rent Concessions**[3], and amenities[4]. Additional data can often be found with online lease listings, but be careful with these. They are not always accurate or up to date.

Although, there are quite a few problems with this survey approach, a valuable rent survey can still be

---

[1] or comparable

[2] For multifamily rental rates per square foot are usually not given. Instead typically the total rent and the size of the apartment in square feet will be given. From there it is easy to calculate the price per square foot by taking the total price and dividing by the square footage of the apartment.

[3] Rent concessions are a discounts and incentives or some other allowance given to the tenant

[4] For multifamily also ask about the number of bedrooms/bathrooms in their apartments and how many of each unit type they have. This is often called the "unit mix".

produced which will give a good **Estimated Market Rent** .

Problems with conducting a rent survey include: What is comparable? Can you reach the owners, managers, and brokers? Will they give you accurate information? Will they include discounts and incentives that they are giving tenants? Even with problems like these a rent survey can be very useful.

A vital question for every rent survey is: What is comparable? As mentioned above, few properties are very comparable. But if a property is at least somewhat similar it is a good one to include in a rent survey. If it has qualities that potential tenants would pay more for, then you can expect the rent to be higher. And if it has qualities that potential tenants would pay less for, then you can expect the rent to be lower. It is a comparison. The more comparable two properties are the closer their rents should be.

After collecting all of this "market rent" data it is time to make sense of it. Create a spreadsheet, like in Microsoft Excel, that includes the following information in columns[1]:

- The top row[2] should show the information for the property being analyzed, also known as the **Subject Property**. It is often a good idea to put this in bold or a different color so it stands out.

---

[1] A column is vertical line of cells

[2] A row is a horizontal line of cells

- The property name and address (note: there may be multiple entries/rows for an address that has multiple spaces for lease)
- Size in square feet of the space for rent
- Lease rate in dollars per square foot (need to be calculated from total rent and size of lease space for multifamily)
- Expense rate per square foot for tenant reimbursed expenses (usually 0 for multifamily)
- Total rate for Lease Rate plus Expense Rate
- List of amenities to be used to judge how comparable a space is

Each row should list one comparable rental space. Include only spaces that are comparable. Then put the properties in order from most comparable to least comparable. The Subject property listed at the top of the spreadsheet should have a market rate closest to the most comparable properties that are listed.

The more comparable properties that are included, the more likely the rent survey will give solid, useful information about market rents. Better properties should have higher rents and lesser properties should have lower rents; so include this information in the estimate of market rent. If done properly and in an open market the comparable rents will tend to be centered around a good estimate of the market rental rate.

Remember this does not have to be perfect. The data will not be perfect but with a good sample size it can give a good estimate of market rental rate.

There are companies out there that maintain statistics like this. However, if using this type of data be sure the comparison is "apples to apples". Often these companies cover different or broader geographical areas and do not take into account true comparability. It is usually a good idea for the investor to complete their own rent survey to ensure a good comparison.

Over time investors familiar with an area develop a good estimate of market rents in their head. They have this from experience conducting formal and informal rent surveys in an area.

Common Area Maintenance (CAM's)

For many leases, the owner is reimbursed for certain expenses. These are often called **Expense Pass Through's** because the expenses are passed through to the tenants. Many of these **Reimbursable Expenses** are often combined into **CAM Charges** or **CAM's**. For all leases it is essential to understand exactly how reimbursed expenses and CAM charges are calculated because they can be a significant amount.

Many leases specify a current CAM charge rate. Then the CAM charges will grow at exactly the same rate as the owner's expenses increase or by some public index like an inflation index or by some other method explicitly described in the lease. Many other leases charge for actual CAM expenses allocated to tenants.

Lease Types - Net Leases

Net leases are leases that have a base rent plus expenses that are reimbursed to the property owner. These **Reimbursed Expenses** must be explicitly stated in the lease. If they are not included in the lease then the tenant does not pay them.

These expenses can include CAM charges, property management fees, property taxes, insurance, reserves, capital expenditures for large items like replacement of air conditioning units, or any other expense the landlord has from operating the property. It is important to understand exactly what expenses are included in the lease terms.

Some owners will charge high management fees or other operational fees that are not very clear why they are included. As an investor it is important to understand that a new tenant may not agree to these in the future. So be sure to understand tenants' reimbursable expenses for net leases.

The key to reimbursed expenses is: The way these expenses are calculated and reimbursed is specified EXACTLY in the lease. The lease explicitly states the expenses that the owner pays and the ones the tenant pays.

For properties that have multiple tenants the expenses are usually **Prorated**. Prorating just means allocating each tenant's fair share of expenses to each one. It is also called their **Pro Rata**" share. It is easiest to understand proration through a simple example. Let's say there is a building with 100,000sf in it. The tenant that leases 20,000sf is leasing 20% (20,000sf / 100,000sf = 20%) of the property so they pay 20 percent of the expenses. Again, this all needs to be specified in the lease contract.

As always, understand all the terms in lease contracts.

Capital Expenditures (CapEx)

The way that expenses for MAJOR items are reimbursed is critical to understand also. Some common examples of major repairs are: roof replacements, air conditioner replacements, and parking lot resurfacing. And there are many others. For example, if a new tenant just moved into a 20 year old building and the owner discovers a new roof is needed. Is this the tenant's or owner's expense? And how much of the expense does the tenant pay? The tenant did not get the benefit of the first 20yrs of the roof and may not get the full benefit of the full future life of the new roof. The only thing that matters is: What does the lease state?

This is a big expense and the lease should say whether it is the tenant's or owner's expense. If the owner has been charging for reserves and keeping a reserve account this is fairly simple to resolve.

Below are some common **Net Lease** terms that are vital to understand. These terms are not always used consistently so when in doubt look at the lease itself. The lease is the only way to completely understand what expenses are paid by the tenant and what expenses are paid by the landlord.

Triple Net (NNN)

Triple Net (NNN) is a very common type of lease agreement. It is commonly used for industrial properties and single tenant retail spaces, like fast food restaurants and large drugstore chains. Generally, the tenant pays rent plus taxes, insurance and maintenance. The landlord is usually responsible for expenses associated with the outside walls, roof, and foundation.

Quadruple Net (NNNN)

Quadruple Net (NNNN) is similar to Triple Net (NNN) but it is a term used when the tenant also pays for the expenses associated with the outside walls, roof, and/or foundation in addition to for taxes, insurance, and maintenance. These are also sometimes called **Absolute Net** because the tenant pays for absolutely all of the expenses. Definitely, look at the contract for the details on this type of lease.

Double Net (NN)

Double Net (NN) is similar to Triple Net (NNN) but the tenant typically pays only rent plus taxes and insurance. The landlord is responsible for maintenance and other expenses.

Single Net

Single Net leases are also used, but not as frequently. These are similar to Double Net (NN) but the tenant typically pays only rent plus taxes. The landlord is responsible for maintenance, insurance expenses, and other expenses.

Single Net leases are also sometimes called Net Leases although most people generically refer to N, NN, NNN, and NNNN leases as "net leases".

Summary of Net Lease Expenses

Lease Type	Taxes	Insurance	Maintenance	Walls / Roof / Foundation
NNNN	Tenant Pays	Tenant Pays	Tenant Pays	Tenant Pays
NNN	Tenant Pays	Tenant Pays	Tenant Pays	Owner Pays
NN	Tenant Pays	Tenant Pays	Owner Pays	Owner Pays
N	Tenant Pays	Owner Pays	Owner Pays	Owner Pays

Lease Types - Gross and Modified Gross Leases

Gross Leases are the easiest to understand. The tenant pays for rent only. The landlord pays for all expenses.

There are also **Modified Gross Leases** where the landlord pays all expenses except for certain specific expenses like electricity. The tenant is responsible for those specific expenses only. Look at the lease to see exactly what expenses the tenant is responsible for with a modified gross lease.

Gross and Modified Gross leases are commonly used in office leasing.

Lease Types - Percentage Leases

Another common type of lease is the **Percentage Lease**. These leases are typically used in retail spaces like in shopping centers where the owner promotes the center and expects to share in high profits when the center does well as a result of the owner's advertising.

Percentage Rent includes a baseline rent plus a percentage of the tenant's sales above a specified amount called the **Breakpoint**. For example if the tenant's sales are $120,000 and the breakpoint is $100,000 then the tenant pays the base rent plus a percentage of $20,000 ($120,000 - $100,000 = $20,000). The percentage must be specified in the lease. The rent over the baseline is often called **Overage Rent**.

Lease Types – Multifamily Leases

Multifamily Leases are very different from the commercial leases discussed above. These are individual residential leases. They are normally between the landlord and an individual or family rather than a business. They rarely include expense reimbursements, except sometimes for utilities like electricity, gas, water, and/or sewer. These reimbursements can be implemented through a **RUBS**[1] program, which is simply a method to prorate utilities across all the tenants[2].

---

[1] RUBS stands for a Resident Utility Billing System

[2] Multifamily units may also be individually metered for natural gas, electricity, and/or water so the tenants pay these expenses directly to the utility company.

These leases are typically short-term: from 1 month to 12 months. 1, 6, and 12 month terms are very common. 1 month leases are commonly called **Month-To-Month Leases** and typically extend one month at a time if the tenant stays. If the tenant gives 30 days notice to vacate then the lease will be terminated at the end of that time.

Since Multifamily properties typically have weak, relatively short-term leases it is important to look at historical income, vacancies, ongoing/recurring expenses, and capital expenditures to estimate how the property will operate in the future. This is because it is relatively easy for a tenant to move out, at any time and create a vacancy. So it is vital to know how the property has been operating historically in order to estimate the future performance.

On the other hand, the shorter, weaker leases have some advantages; it is easier to raise rents as rental rates increase over time and leases expire.

Another notable difference in these leases is that the residential rental laws do apply here and tend to protect and favor the tenant. The idea here is that residential tenants are not necessarily sophisticated investors and so there are laws to protect them from possibly unscrupulous landlords. It may or may not be reasonable, but that seems to be how the laws are written. Residential leases tend to be much weaker leases. So as an owner, the historical income and expenses are a much better indicator of the future than the strength of the leases.

Parking

Parking can be a common source of problems. Leases often specify how many spots are allocated to tenants and any limitations. It is a good idea to make sure there is enough parking to avoid conflicts between tenants. Remember good parking helps make contented customers, who tend to make contented tenants, who tend to make contented investors.

Some properties will have agreements with neighboring properties to share parking which is commonly referred to as a **Reciprocal Parking Agreement**. This type of agreement may improve or worsen the parking. However, usually these agreements help because they provide more parking and parking peaks are effectively averaged out over a larger lot. Be aware of any parking agreements.

Rentable, Usable, and Common Areas

When a tenant leases a space there is a specific number of square feet inside their leased area that they have exclusive use to. In other words, nobody else can use it. By definition, the area for exclusive use of the tenants in a building is called the **Usable Area** of the building.

The remaining area in a building is called a **Common Area** or shared area. The common area is composed of spaces like hallways, bathrooms, elevator lobbies, mechanical rooms, and electrical rooms that are shared by all the tenants[1].

The total of the "useable area" of the building plus the "common area" is called the **Rentable Area**. One way to think of the rentable area is to think of it as the total square footage of the building.

Rentable(sf) = Useable (sf) + Common Area(sf)
Total(sf) = Tenant(sf) + Shared (sf)

There is no need to memorize these different formulas. They are included only to help with understanding. Once they are understood. They are fairly intuitive. However, it is important to remember the definitions of Rentable, Useable, and Common areas. These terms are usually used in Office spaces and sometimes in Industrial spaces.

Depending on the geographic region of a property there are two commonly used ways to account for this "shared or common area": the Efficiency Factor and Load Factor

Efficiency Factor

Some regions use a term called **Efficiency** or **Efficiency Factor**. This factor is simply the ratio of useable (tenant area) to rentable (total area) square footage in a building.

---

[1] For multi-tenant buildings the major vertical floor penetrations like elevator shafts, vents, and stairways are typically not included in square footage. However, these may be included for a single tenant building.

Efficiency = Useable(sf) / Rentable(sf)
   is normally smaller than 1

The useable area (tenant area) is typically smaller than the rentable area (total area) so this ratio is less than 1 (or equal[1]). It is usually just slightly less than 1, like 0.9614 = 96.14%.

What Efficiency Means

The **Efficiency** is the percentage of useable area (tenant area) out of the rentable area (total area) of a building. So an efficiency of 95% means that 95% of the total area (rentable area) is for the exclusive use of tenants (useable area) and 5% (100% - 95% = 5%) of the building is in the common or shared area. The meaning rather than the math is what is important to understand.

Load Factor or Add-On Factor

Other regions use a term called a **Load Factor**, **Load**, or **Add-On Factor**. This factor is simply the ratio of Rentable area (total area) to Usable area (tenant area) of a building.

Load Factor = Add-On Factor
   = Rentable(sf) / Useable(sf)
   is normally larger than 1

The rentable area (total area) is larger than the useable area (tenant area) so this ratio is always greater than 1 (or equal[2]). It is usually just slightly over 1, like 1.0485.

---

[1] Technically, they could be equal so the ratio would equal 1

[2] Technically, they could be equal so the ratio would equal 1

What Load Factor Means

The **Load Factor** or **Add-On Factor** is how many times more the rentable area (total square feet) is than the useable area (tenant square feet). This is the "factor" that the tenant's usable area is multiplied by to calculate the rentable area. It shows how much is added on for common area rent. This is why it is also called an "add-on" factor.

For example, a load factor of 1.05 means that the rentable area (total area) is 105% (1.05 = 105%) of the useable area (tenant area). In other words, 5% is added-on to the tenant's useable area to calculate actual rent charged. Again, the meaning rather than the math is what is important to understand.

Using the Efficiency and Load Factor

Why go through all this explanation? Well landlords can charge tenants their prorated share of the common areas and they use Efficiency and Load Factors to easily calculate how much to allocate to each tenant. As always, this would have to be specified in the lease. And usually, this will apply only to office buildings and sometimes industrial spaces.

The discussion up to this point has been for calculating the Efficiency or Load Factor for the entire building. This is the same factor that will be applied to each tenant's usable space to allocate the common area rents to each tenant.

The landlord normally charges for the Rentable area. This "charged for" area is the tenant's personal useable area **plus** their prorated share of the common area rents. It is calculated as follows:

Rentable(sf)=Useable(tenants area) xLoad Factor
= Useable (sf of tenants area) / Efficiency

Also note that:

Load Factor = 1 / Efficiency

They are the "inverse" of each other.

The Rentable square footage is what the landlord collects rent on. This is greater than the tenant's area (usable area)[1]. It is the useable plus prorated common area rent. In this way the landlord collects each tenant's prorated share of the rent for the common areas.

Of course none of this applies for a building with only one tenant (Single Tenant Building), because there are no shared areas. All of the hallways, bathrooms, elevator lobbies, mechanical rooms, and electrical rooms are leased by and charged to the single tenant.

Also, this concept of useable vs. rentable is usually only used in office leases and sometimes in industrial.

---

[1] Because Load Factor is ≥ 1 and 1/ Efficiency is ≥ 1. Technically, they could be equal if these ratios equal 1.

Chapter 5 - The Sale:
Where the Rubber Hits the Road

Purchasing income-producing commercial real estate can be exciting and nerve-racking at the same time. If the investor has done all the research and understands the investment property it should be a much less stressful and more rewarding experience.

Letter of Intent or Letter of Interest (LOI)

Many real estate investment purchases start with a Letter of Intent/Interest (LOI). This is typically just a "gentleman's agreement". It is usually written so that it is not binding which means it is not yet a contractual promise or obligation. Instead it shows an **Intent** or **Interest** to buy. It is the starting point for developing a binding offer.

So why even use it? Actually, it is an incredibly valuable tool to negotiate a sale. It shows the seller the **basic** terms under which the buyer would like to purchase the property. It clearly shows the buyer's intent. It is signed by the buyer in order to show intent even though it is not binding. The seller can accept it "as-is" or request changes to the LOI by writing out a list of requested changes, signing this list, and submitting it back to the buyer[1]. This would also be signed to show intent. The signatures are not binding but are included to show this is the true intent of the buyer and seller and to avoid misunderstandings.

The buyer and seller go back and forth with modifications until an agreement is made or they decide they cannot reach an agreement. Additionally, if there are multiple LOI's this process gives the seller a way to compare the different ones.

A primary reason the LOI is so valuable, is that it starts to document in writing what the buyer and seller plan to agree on in the actual sale contract. It provides a way to start documenting the agreement without making a binding contractual agreement. It is a great tool for both the buyer and seller to figure out how the deal can work.

The LOI has the basic terms of sale that the buyer is proposing. It typically will include important **Deal Points** like the proposed sale price (Strike Price), down payment, financing intentions, time to conduct due diligence, and time until the sale is completed or closed. It can include anything the buyer considers important for the opening round of negotiations.

It also identifies the buyer so the seller can make their own determination of whether the buyer has the

---

[1] This is essentially an offer / counteroffer situation.

capability and real intent to buy the property. This is one reason the buyer's reputation is important.

Qualifying Buyers and Sellers

Qualifying potential buyers and sellers is very important at this stage. There are buyers who do not have the resources and/or experience to buy a property, but they will make an offer. This is the time to investigate if they truly intend to buy the property and are capable. This is commonly called **Qualifying** them.

If there are any indications that the buyer does not really intend to buy the property or does not have the capability to follow through, then the seller should not accept the LOI. Or the seller can ask for additional terms to make it more difficult for the buyer to back out if the LOI is accepted. The buyer's response to this will give an indication of their seriousness.

Once the property is under contract the seller usually cannot take other offers that may be better and may be more likely to close. The property is **Tied-Up** because other offers cannot be accepted until the current offer expires or fails. This can waste a lot of precious time; so it is usually better to accept only solid offers that have a good chance of completion.

It is also important to know whether a seller is serious about selling a property or if they are just "fishing". **Fishing** means they are just throwing something out there to see who "bites". Sometimes they just want to gauge where the market is, but most of the time they will sell if the "right" offer comes along. Usually, this means that they are looking for someone willing to pay an inflated price.

It is probably best to avoid people who are not serious about completing a sale. They often will be difficult to work with because they are not motivated and will not compromise much. They will probably be a waste of time in the end. It is a good idea to qualify buyers and sellers early in any transaction.

Purchase and Sale Agreement (PSA)

Another enormous benefit of an "agreed to" LOI is that it can easily be transformed into a **Purchase and Sale Agreement (PSA)**. The LOI has the basic terms of the agreement. The PSA contract takes the LOI to the next logical step by explicitly detailing ALL of the terms of the sales agreement. It is a formal **Offer To Purchase**. Since all of the terms[1] are in this agreement there may be a need for changes and negotiations to finalize it; however, it should not need many modifications because the LOI agreement was already agreed on. This contract is simply a list of all the terms of the sales agreement or contract. The PSA becomes a binding contractual agreement once it is signed by all parties (executed).

Just like leasing, it is all in the contract. If it is not written down in the contract do no rely on it!

---

[1] Not just the basic terms as in the LOI

Offers & Counter Offers

The initial PSA contract is often considered the actual buyer's **Offer**[1]. The seller can accept this offer by signing it. If this happens there is an executed and binding contract. Or they may ask for changes with a signed **Counter Offer** or **Counter**. The other party can accept this by signing the "counter" or counter offering again with more requested changes. This process of "counter offering" goes on until both parties agree to and sign the last counter offer.

Typically, it is best to make the counter offer so that it includes the previous offer/counteroffer(s) and just lists the requested changes. This makes it easier to negotiate to an agreement so that all deal points do not need to be renegotiated with every counter offer. Previously agreed on points do not need to be revisited. Typically, just the changes or additions need to be negotiated.

A crucial point to understand is that when a counter offer is made then the previous offer/counteroffer is no longer binding. The latest counter offer becomes binding and executed when both parties agree to and sign it.

"Tying-Up" a Property

Once a property is under contract it is **Tied-Up**. This term for **Tying-Up** a Property" is commonly used because the buyer and the seller are not free to do anything they want. They have a contractual

---

[1] The LOI can be considered the initial offer, however it is not binding. It is really a tool to get to the initial offer, which is the PSA contract.

obligation to each other according to the PSA contract.

An important question that every seller should find an answer to is: Does the potential buyer have the capability, resources, and true intent to purchase the property? If this is not the case, then the seller should not sign the PSA. This will "tie up" the property and keep the seller from negotiating with other potential buyers who may be more serious and likely to close the purchase.

It is fairly obvious that this is important when selling a property, but its importance is less obvious when making an offer on a property. Remember, only serious offers are considered earnestly in most cases. If an offer looks sloppy or weak it may not get full consideration.

Negotiating Deal Points

The **Strike Price** or property sale price is an important **Deal Point** and is often negotiated from the amount first shown on the LOI. However, it is critical to not focus on this as the **only** deal point. There are many others and very often one side cannot bend far from their Strike Price but they can on other important points that may make a deal happen. As an example, let's say the buyer cannot go above a $2M price and the seller does not want to go that low. Sometimes the problem can be solved with a bigger down payment, a shorter time to complete the sale, or even some creative financing with the seller carrying[1] part of the loan.

Anytime there seems to be a stalemate on a specific deal point, try to think of another way to solve the problem by changing other deal points. Very often this can solve the issue. Avoid getting "tunnel vision" where the focus is on specific points, instead of the deal as a whole.

Escrow

Escrow is a way to manage the sale process so both the seller's and buyer's interests are protected. Escrow gives the buyer and the seller the time necessary to do all the work required to make the sale transaction happen.

Escrow is when a neutral third-party[2], called an **Escrow Holder**, is asked to manage the entire sales transaction from start to finish. They are trusted to be unbiased, to hold and disburse the funds in the transaction, and to carry out the instructions delineated in the PSA. The **Escrow Instructions** are typically generated from the executed PSA contract. They are the "directions" that the escrow holder must follow. No changes can be made to these directions unless a written request is made and signed by both the buyer and the seller.

---

[1] The seller "carrying" part of the loan means they are loaning part of the **Purchase Money** to the buyer by not being paid immediately. The buyer is borrowing the money from the seller. This is also known as a **Seller Carryback**.

[2] Third-party means not involved directly in the transaction. They are expected to be neutral and unbiased.

Escrow is normally **opened** or started with the escrow holder once a PSA contract is executed[1]. Initial deposits as agreed to in the PSA are made with the escrow holder.

The escrow period gives the buyer time to do all their research, also called **Due Diligence**, about the property, find financing, and get everything done that is necessary to complete the sale.

In some states the escrow holder is an **Escrow Company** that manages the entire escrow while other states use attorneys or other companies to manage escrow. The entity managing the escrow must always follow all of directions in the PSA. They also hold funds during escrow, make sure all necessary paperwork is completed and signed, make necessary public filings/recordings, and disburse funds at the end of escrow. They are a "Clearing House" for the entire transaction.

The **Escrow Period** is a very important deal point. Commercial escrows in very unusual circumstances can be as short as a couple of days, but in practice are usually 30 to 90 days. For development or land sales, escrows of 6 months to 1.5 years or more are common[2]. Escrow is **Closed** when all of the terms of the PSA have been fulfilled, the sale is recorded with the county, and everything is paid off. This includes paying the taxes, insurance, escrow fees, legal fees, outstanding loan amounts,

---

[1] Agreed to and signed by all involved parties

[2] Developing a property from raw land takes more time to research and finalize plans so the escrows are typically longer.

broker commissions, and of course the proceeds of the sale to the seller.

The sales proceeds are typically transferred to the seller just prior to the **Close of Escrow**. Typically, everyone is not paid until near the close of escrow, including the seller. This is a big reason it is such a crucial time.

Due Diligence

Due Diligence is the all of the research that should be reasonably done prior to purchasing any property. This research should include reviewing and understanding all of the known information that shows the history and current state of the real estate. It includes information that the seller provides, reports that the buyer orders, and any research the buyer performs. This can be a substantial amount of work.

If the buyer finds some problem with the property that they were not aware of when they signed the PSA contract, then they can state in writing to the escrow holder that they are not continuing with the sale. If this happens, their deposit money is normally returned. Expenses that are listed specifically in the contract may be deducted from this deposit.

Many people in this business will also call all the written historical documentation, **Due Diligence**. This documentation is often anything from a few sheets of paper to boxes of paperwork.

Due diligence materials[1] can include environmental reports, appraisals, prior sales

---

[1] Due diligence materials are also called just due diligence

documentation, and anything that the current owner knows about or should know about the property. The owner should provide ALL information known about the property and hold NOTHING back. If the owner withholds any information it could cause the deal to fall apart or be the source of a lawsuit in the future. This is a time to be completely honest and let the buyer make their own conclusions.

The PSA should specify how much time the seller has to provide the due diligence materials. It is often a few days or up to a week from the date the PSA is signed. It is a good idea to state in the PSA that all dates will slip one day for every day that the due diligence material is provided late. This incentivizes the seller to provide the materials on time and gives the buyer time to review them.

To protect themselves, the seller should always make a **written** list of all due diligence materials provided to the buyer. This list should include a name for each piece of the due diligence material, a date, and at least enough information to identify each item. It should also include a signature line so when the due diligence material is provided to the buyer they sign and acknowledge the exact material provided and the date it was received. This helps avoid misunderstandings and claims in the future that something was not provided. As always, get it in writing and get it signed.

Due Diligence Period

The **Due Diligence Period** is the amount of time that the potential buyer is given to review the due diligence materials. This is a very important time period. It allows the buyer a chance to research and evaluate the property and make sure it is as it appears. Depending on how the PSA contract is written the potential buyer can acknowledge the completion of the due diligence by letting the due diligence period lapse or state it is completed in writing. It all depends on the wording in the contract, so be sure to understand this part of the PSA.

Typically at the end of a successful due diligence period the deposit or some other amount of money becomes non-refundable. A common term for this step is the money has **Gone Hard**[1]. This cash will normally remain in the escrow holder's account until escrow closes.

Remember, escrow can close with a completed sale or not. Usually, if the sale is completed the money that has "gone hard" will be applied towards the purchase price at the close of escrow. However, if the sale fails to complete, the PSA contract should explicitly state how escrow will be closed including the disbursement of funds. This is very important to have in the PSA contract. If the sale is not completed the money that has "gone hard" is usually disbursed to the seller as liquidated damages at the close of escrow.

There are some cases where the money will **Pass-Through** immediately to the seller at the end of the due diligence period or some other specified time. However, this is not the norm and is usually only used

---

[1] Do not confuse this with a hard money loan, which will be discussed in the chapter on Financing.

in development deals with very long escrows or other unusual circumstances.

Remember, that during the due diligence period the buyer can withdraw from the sale for almost any reason and usually get all or most of the deposit back. Satisfying the due diligence contingency is a big step towards completing the sale transaction because it usually will cost the buyer money to withdraw after the due diligence is satisfied.

Free Look Period

The term **Free Look Period** is sometimes used. This means there is a PSA contract that allows the buyer some specific period of time, called the Free Look Period, to research a property before any money is committed. This is not really in the seller's best interests and normally this is not recommended unless there is some justifiable reason for it.

Contingencies

Typically, there are **Contingencies** written into a PSA. A contingency is just a condition that must be satisfied for the sale to proceed forward. These contingencies must be met by a date specified in the contract. The contract must state how these contingencies are to be satisfied. It also needs to specify whether the contingency is met just by a date expiring or if it must be met by a signed statement provided to the escrow holder. It needs to be specified in the contract as always.

The due diligence is one contingency that must be met for the sale to continue forward. It must be completed according to the contract or the sale will stop.

There are quite a few other possible contingencies. Anything that both the buyer and the seller agree to make a condition of the sale can be written into the contract as a contingency. Any contingency needs to have a date to be satisfied by, how it will be satisfied, and what happens if it is not satisfied. A couple of common contingencies are:

- **Financing Contingency** - Financing must be found
- **Environmental Contingency** - Environmental report must find no significant problems
- **Physical Inspection Contingency** - The property must be in satisfactory physical condition

If the sale is not completed because a contingency is not satisfied the PSA needs to be very specific on what happens to the buyer's deposit and how is escrow ended. How is the deposit disbursed? When is escrow closed? These are very important questions to have answers to. It is much easier to agree to these ahead of time when the PSA is written than while a sale is falling apart.

Phase I and Phase II Environmental Reports

A **Phase I Environmental Analysis or Report** is often called just a **Phase I**. It is a report from a third-party[1] company who specializes in investigating and reporting the environmental condition of a property. This is called a Phase I because it is a first level investigation. It usually includes a thorough visual property inspection[2] and research on the property history. If no problems are found or suspected in the Phase I then the environmental contingency is usually met.

However, if the Phase I shows that there may be environmental issues then a second level Phase II is typically required. A Phase II investigation usually includes taking and analyzing samples of dirt and/or water from the property. Holes are usually drilled to take the samples so there is quite a bit of additional work. For this reason the Phase II inspections typically costs quite a bit more than the Phase I.

A Phase I may not be required if the buyer is convinced there are no problems. However, it is usually best to conduct a Phase I report just to protect the buyer. Also a Phase II may be ordered without the Phase I if a property is known to have environmental issues or if it has **Underground Storage Tanks**[3], like for a gas station; or if it has been a dry cleaner for many years.

Environmental reports state the results of the investigation and typically guarantee the results the company has investigated and believe to be true. They essentially act like environmental insurance. As

---

[1] Third-party means not involved directly in the transaction. They are expected to be neutral and unbiased.

[2] with photographs taken

[3] In environment reports **Underground Storage Tanks** are abbreviated as **UST** and **Leaking Underground Storage Tanks** are abbreviated as **LUST**

expected, these typically do not guarantee anything the environmental company cannot substantiate or investigate properly.

Physical Condition of the Property

Investigating the **Physical Condition** of the property is critical. Is the building well-built and well-maintained? There is a long list of things to check that include:

- Are the foundation and walls in good condition?
- Is there a history of roof leaks? When was the roof last replaced? Is there any remaining warranty on the roof and can it be transferred to a new owner? Does water drain from the roof or do puddles of water stand?
- Is there a history of any plumbing supply problems, especially slab leaks[1], wall leaks, or other leaks? Are there any problems with the sewer?
- Is there a history of any electrical/power supply problems?
- Does water drain properly outside?
- Is there enough parking for the property usage?
- Is there a history of air conditioner / boiler problems? How old are the units?

This is just a partial list of important answers to get when purchasing a property. Also, it is highly

---

[1] Slab Leaks are leaks in pipes that are inside a cement slab. These can be difficult to find and expensive to repair. Also, if the building has a history of slab leaks the buyer should be aware it could be likely to have more.

recommended to hire a third-party building inspection company that specializes in evaluating the physical condition of **commercial** buildings. They are experts at investigating the physical condition and may notice many things that the investor could miss.

"Cheap is Expensive"

There is an expression, "Cheap is Expensive". The environmental and physical Inspections normally cost thousands of dollars each. This can seem expensive. But they protect the buyer from potential losses in the future that can be substantial. If no inspections are done and any major unforeseen[1] problems occur then it is the buyer's problem. Saving that few thousand dollars on inspections could cost much, much more in the future!

It is like an insurance policy. Spending thousands of dollars to protect an investment worth hundreds of thousands to millions of dollars seems like a good price for the piece of mind. Also, the inspection reports typically guarantee their inspections. They may have lots of exceptions and disclaimers for anything they could not reasonably investigate, but if they just miss something then they are typically responsible.

Long Escrows and Long Contingency Periods

If a buyer asks for an unusually long escrow period, due diligence period, or other contingency

---

[1] Unforeseen by everyone. The seller and the broker have the obligation to tell the buyer of any known problems.

period this should concern the seller. It could be a warning that they are not very serious. If they want an excessively long time to complete the sale there should be a valid and easily explained reason. If there is not, then "let the seller[1] beware".

Ownership Entities

There are a number of ways to hold ownership of a property. The type of **Ownership Entity** chosen and the setup of it has many legal and tax implications that should be discussed with an attorney and tax advisor. To set up an ownership entity it is highly recommended to hire an attorney, who specializes in setting these up. This can avoid costly mistakes and delays.

Start an investigation into the preferred type of ownership as early as possible. The type of ownership will depend on the specific circumstances. Do not wait until the last minute to setup the ownership entity or there may be problems at the close of escrow when it is time to transfer ownership. Some of these entities take some time to set-up.

Sole Proprietor

The simplest type of ownership is the **Sole Proprietor**. This is a type of ownership where an individual directly owns the property. Even though this is not a separate entity, it still has tax and legal consequences so it is important to speak with an attorney and tax advisor.

---

[1] Not the buyer

General Partnership (GP)

Another type of ownership is a **General Partnership**(GP). These are typically regulated by each state and so will vary from one state to another. This type of ownership requires at least two partners. Each is called a general partner, all share equally in the management of the property, and each has complete liability for all debts of the partnership no matter how much is invested. This is probably not a good entity for larger groups or people who do not know each other well because disagreements on how to manage the property can be difficult to resolve. It also exposes all of the partners to full liability. Use an attorney to set this up.

Limited Liability Partnerships (LLP)

Limited Liability Partnerships (LLP) are another way to own a property. Like the General Partnership this requires at least two partners. However, a major difference from the general partnership is that one partner is the **General Partner**. This partner manages the business and the partnership and assumes unlimited liability for the LLP. The other partners are passive and take no part in the management of the LLP and have limited liability to just the amount they have at risk in the partnership.

The partnership has a date that it will be dissolved. Consequently it has a finite life, so make sure that this lifetime allows enough time to do whatever is planned for the property. This type of ownership is good when more centralized management is useful. Again, use an attorney to set this up properly.

C-Corporation

A **C-Corporation** is an entity that has its own tax and legal identity. This is the same structure that public companies use. It is a separate entity from the owner(s) and has its own Tax ID number[1].

It is owned by its shareholders and generally provides limited liability for them. This ownership entity must have an annual shareholders' meeting and must have separate tax returns filed and paid. These and some other corporate formalities must be followed, so it does take a little work to maintain.

It is highly recommended that an attorney who specializes in setting up corporations is used to create this type of entity. This does take some time to create so plan ahead.

S-Corporation

An **S-Corporation** is very similar to the C-Corporation but it is not a separate tax entity. Taxes from this type of property "flow through" and are reported on the shareholder(s) tax returns. This not a common ownership entity for investors, because income from real estate rentals is severely limited by tax laws.

Limited Liability Company (LLC)

Limited Liability Company (LLC) is another ownership option. These are typically regulated by

---

[1] A Tax ID number is like an individual's Social Security number but for a company.

each state and so will vary from one state to another. It is like a corporation but has fewer "Corporate Formalities" so it is easier to run. It provides limited liability to its shareholders and all members can be active in the management of the company. The LLC has fewer restrictions on members and generally is a very flexible form of ownership.

This is a common ownership entity for commercial properties. It is commonly used when there are only a few owners or even one. Again, use an attorney to set this up properly.

Tenant-in-Common (TIC)

Tenant-in-Common (TIC) ownership is not an ownership entity, but it is another common way of owning a property. It is when there are multiple owners who each own an **Undivided Fractionalized Interest** in a property. Fractionalized means they each own some percentage of the property. However, Undivided means they each own a percentage[1] of the "entire" property and cannot divide up the property into parts. In other words, they cannot say, "that part is yours, this part is mine". They all own a fraction of the entire property.

TIC's are often sold as a way for a smaller investor to get into a larger, higher quality property. The investor still needs to do their research and make sure the investment will work for them and their particular circumstances.

---

[1] The percentages of ownership do not have to be equal.

Chapter 6 - Performance Metrics:
"The Numbers"

"The Numbers" tell so much about a property. Is it a good deal? What is it worth? Can it be made better? Any analysis of a commercial real estate investment should include the numbers. The price paid, down payment, loan payments, income, and expenses all affect the "bottom line" of how much money the investment makes. This is why people make the investment to start with. "The numbers" tell a big part of the story.

Measuring Performance of an Investment

What is a good investment? This is a great question but not so easy to answer. There is no shortage of opinions of ways to figure out if an investment is good or not.

This chapter focuses on "the numbers" of an investment. Each investment has a huge amount of "numbers" associated with it. There is the income for each tenant each month. There are the expenses for each expense item for each month. This is a huge amount of information when you consider that all of this data comes in month after month. Somehow there needs to be a way to make sense out of what seems to be an overwhelming amount of data.

Fortunately there is. There are **metrics** and **statistics**[1] that investors use to take huge amounts of data and distill it down to a few numbers that can be compared across different investments. This comparison helps investors decide what is a good investment for their own particular set of circumstances.

Income

The **Gross Scheduled Income (GSI)** is sometimes called the **Potential Rental Income (PRI)**. It is the total income that is expected if all space is leased and there are no losses to vacancies or collection problems. In other words it is the "best case scenario" expected for rental income. The value can be given as "per month" or "per year" but be careful to be consistent in all calculations. "Per year" numbers are commonly used because they will average out seasonal differences and give a more realistic description of the property.

---

[1] A **metric** is a way to make a measurement, which can then be used to compare against another measurement. A **statistic** is just a number that has been calculated from a large amount of data where this number summarizes the data. For example, a commonly used statistic is an average.

Rent Roll

The **Rent Roll** is a great starting point for any investigation into a commercial property because it is a "snapshot" of the tenants in the property at a point in time. This snapshot should be now or very recently. An old rent roll shows how the property "used to be", but is not very useful now. Usually the owner of a property will provide a **Current Rent Roll**. It is a list of tenants and basic information about the space they are leasing. The rent roll should show a list of the tenants, the spaces they are renting, lease starting and end dates, the size of the spaces, the rental rates (price per sf), total rents, and notes about the tenants. This is easiest to see in rows and columns in a table or spreadsheet. It also shows current vacancies because if a space is shown that has no tenant then it is vacant.

The rents in the rent roll can be added up to see income and/or potential income. Also, the lease starting and end dates show if tenants are on longer term leases or shorter term. It also shows when leases expire and so when the landlord will need to renew a lease or find a new tenant.

Sample Rent Roll:

Tenants	Unit#	Unit sf	Rental Rate	Total Rent	Lease End /Start	Notes
Tenant 1	A	2,542 sf	$1.45	$3,686/mo	06/01/xx 05/31/xx	
Tenant 2	B1	1,654 sf	$1.50	$2,481/mo	12/01/xx 11/30/xx	
Tenant 3	B2	1,287 sf	$1.20	$1,544/mo	04/30/xx 03/31/xx	

. . . and so on for other tenants

Lease Abstract

A lease abstract is very similar to a rent roll, but it usually includes many more lease details and takes more time to create. The idea is to put into a table or spreadsheet the significant details of the leases. This requires going through each lease and pulling out the noteworthy details. This can be a time consuming endeavor, but will reveal a lot about the tenants and the property.

Other Income

Other income may be received from parking charges or fees for other services provided. For multifamily properties other income often comes from coin operated laundry facilities, garages, parking fees, and extra storage space fees.

Vacancy and Vacancy Factor

Vacancy is when a space is not rented and so does not generate any income during the time it is unfilled. It reduces the income from the amount possible shown in the Gross Scheduled Income (GSI). Since the goal of the owner is typically to minimize unrented space and maximize income they will try to rent it out as soon at possible.

Knowing that a particular property at a particular moment has 8,000sf vacant and is not getting the $12,000/sf/month it should, does not give the full picture. However if the owner has an idea of whether it will be rented almost immediately or will take some time is very useful information. The **Vacancy Factor** is a way to show a historical or market average of vacancies so a prediction on the future income can be estimated.

A **Vacancy Factor** is an estimated percentage of Gross Scheduled Income (GSI) that is lost due to expected vacancies. The key here is it is "estimated" and will be used to predict future vacancy rates. Remember the statement, "past performance is no guarantee of future performance"; this is an estimate. However, it can be a very good one.

It can be based on a historical average for the property or some kind of market average. This factor is not often evaluated precisely. It is usually just a rough estimate because it is usually difficult to come to a precise number.

Experienced investors usually have a good idea of what is a reasonable vacancy factor estimate for a given property in a given market. An estimate of 5%

is very common for an average rental market; while 7% to 20% or more is common for a slow rental market; and 2 to 3% for a very busy rental market. Many analyses that are out there will use 5% because they don't really know the market average.

It is very unlikely to have a 0% vacancy factor because as tenants move out and are replaced there is almost always some time needed to find a new tenant and get the space ready. It is very rare that one tenant will move out one day and a new tenant will move in the next. For this reason, there is some time that the space is not rented and so this is "in-effect" a vacancy.

Some quick calculations will illustrate this point. If it takes on average only 2 months to find a replacement tenant every 3 years this is 2 months out of 36 months (3 years) which is about a 5.6% vacancy rate ($2/36 \approx 5.6\%$). Or if it takes 3 months to find a replacement tenant every 5yrs this is a 5% vacancy rate ($3/60 = 5\%$). 2 or 3 months (or more) to find a new tenant is very common in a decent rental market. It can be more in a slower market or if many TI's are required. As you can see it is very easy to have a 5% vacancy rate just due to turnovers in tenants.

This is just for one tenant, but tenants will be moving in and out periodically. Some will renew leases and some will not so there will be an **average** developed over time. This is what the vacancy factor is expressing. Remember that as the length of the lease term increases the amount of time to find a replacement tenant tends to increase also. So long leases do not necessarily guarantee low vacancy factors.

Be careful if an analysis shows a low vacancy factor in a market that is known to have high vacancy rates. Do some research and be sure to use a vacancy rate that makes sense in any analysis.

Remember, a property that is poorly maintained and poorly managed is likely to have a higher vacancy rate than the market it is in. Many tenants do not like to rent in a run-down and poorly run building. This makes a property more difficult to lease which usually increases vacancies.

A property with high actual vacancies may be a reflection of the market that it is in, but it could also be because of poor management, deferred maintenance, or other problems. It is difficult to change the market, but if the problems are with the property itself and can be easily fixed this could be a great deal for an investor. The investor may be able to fix the problems, reduce vacancies, and in turn increase the income.

Credit or Collection Losses

Credit or Collection Losses are when rent that is owed is not paid for whatever reason. This happens when a tenant goes out of business or just does not pay their rent. They are in default on their lease and can be sued for the rent, but this does not help if they just do not have the money.

In most analyses of a property the Credit or Collection Losses are lumped in with the Vacancy Factor whether they state it explicitly or not. It is sometimes called a **Vacancy and Credit Loss Factor**, which really is a better description for it.

However, much of the time people will just call it a **Vacancy Factor**.

Expenses

Building owners will incur expenses running and maintaining a building. Some landlords complicate expenses because they have two sets of expenses; one is for income taxes and one is for selling a property. For the tax version they may include all sorts of expenses that they may not include in their financial analysis when selling a property. Whether this is reasonable or not is a good question for a tax advisor and each individual makes their own decision on how they will operate their investments. The question is what should be included in expenses and what should not when evaluating a property. This section will discuss commonly accepted expenses.

Operational Expenses

Operational Expenses are just the day-to-day operating expenses from running a property. These are also referred to as **Recurring Expenses**. These include property taxes, insurance, maintenance, trash collection, utilities[1] and management fees. There may be other expenses incurred like employees, marketing fees, postage, cell phones, and many others, but it depends on the owner and how they run the property.

Sometimes operational expenses are reimbursed by the tenant through **Expense Pass-Through's**, but only as specified in the leases. Any other expenses

---

[1] Utilities may be individually or separately metered so the tenant pays these expensed directly to the utility provider.

not reimbursed to the property owner are paid for by the property owner. Read the leases!

As mentioned before, **Common Area Maintenance** charges **(CAM Charges or CAM's)** are often a combined expense pass-through to the tenant.

Sometimes a property owner "self manages" property(ies). This does NOT mean there is no management expense. It just means that owner is investing their own time for management. A new owner would have to hire a new property manager or invest their time. Always, include a realistic property management expense in any analysis.

Capital Expenditures (CapEx)

Capital Expenditures (CapEx) should be differentiated from operational expenses. Capital Expenditures are typically large cost maintenance items that are incurred fairly infrequently. Some common examples are replacement of roofs, air conditioning units and boilers, and pavement in parking lots.

These expenses are long term expenses and so are not normally included in the day-to-day operational expenses. They are one-time expenses rather than recurring.

There are cases where it may not be clear "what is a Capital Expenditure" and "what is a normal operating expense". An example of this is if an air conditioning unit needs a rebuild or if roof repairs are required. Which type of expenses these are will depend on the landlord and the lease contracts.

Although Capital Expenditures are not included in operational expenses, they are still very important. When evaluating a property there are lots of questions that should be asked related to capital expenses, like: "Is there a replacement reserve account and will it be transferred in a sale"? How long has it been since the air conditioners, boilers, roof, and parking lot have been replaced? Have there been many maintenance repairs recently? If these items are old or are being repaired frequently there may be a capital expense coming soon. It is good to be aware of these things when analyzing a building.

If the roof, air conditioner, boiler, or pavement has been recently replaced then it will probably be in good working order for a while. However, it is a good idea to ask if there is a warranty and if it can be transferred to a new owner. Warranties are often transferrable and so are often very valuable to a buyer.

Net Operating Income (NOI)

Net Operating Income (NOI) is simply the total income received (in a specific year) less vacancies and credit losses for that year, plus any other income from things like parking fees.

Gross Scheduled Income (GSI)

- Vacancy/Credit Losses

+ Other Income

<u>- Operating Expenses</u>

= NOI

The following expenses are NOT included with operational expenses for these NOI calculations:

- Capital Expenses
- Income Taxes
- Loan Payments (Debt Service, Principal & Interest)
- Reserves
- Tenant Improvements

NOI is one of the most important numbers to understand when evaluating an investment property. It is often calculated incorrectly by people unfamiliar with commercial property investment analysis and can lead to very misleading conclusions.

To be clear: Net operating income does **NOT** mean **ALL** the income actually received. It is all the income actually received **LESS** expenses. There are many cases where someone unfamiliar with commercial properties shows NOI as income without the expenses subtracted off. This is a novice mistake. It will make professional investors and brokers know the person doing the analysis is a beginner.

Capitalization Rate or Cap Rate

The **Capitalization Rate** or **Cap Rate** is calculated by taking the NOI and dividing it by the total amount invested to purchase the property:

Cap Rate = NOI / Cash Invested

The Cap Rate is normally stated as a percentage. Like 6% or 15%. Remember this is just a snapshot of a given period of time. It is usually last year or the 12 months just before the analysis was completed. If anything changes so does this number.

Using Cap Rates

There are a couple of ways to use cap rates and this can cause some confusion when someone is first learning.

One way to think of the cap rate is that it can give an estimate of the "expected" first year income based on historical numbers. This is a prediction or estimate only. Completing a little algebra on the above equation gives:

NOI = Cap Rate x Cash Invested

In other words, if the cap rate is multiplied by the investment it gives an estimate of the income expected. It is in essence an estimate of the first years return in percentage of investment.

Remember this is using historical numbers to an estimate future income. Anything could change, like vacancies, rental rates, and the general condition of the rental market which would change the future cap rate. Remember, "past performance is no guarantee of future performance". It could be better or could be worse. If an investor sees a way to improve the cap rate then it could be a good investment.

Another way to use the cap rate is to compare the cap rate of one property to another. With all else equal a property with a higher cap rate should earn better returns. This comparison can be made between a property and a market cap rate also. Market cap rates can be difficult to determine precisely. However, by investigating many comparable properties in an area an investor will get a sense of what the market cap rate is. This generally comes with experience. Seasoned investors and brokers know reasonable cap rates for a given property type in a given area. A broker can be a great person to ask this kind of information.

There is yet another interpretation for cap rates. There is a concept that there is normally a tradeoff between **Risk vs. Return**. Open markets tend to pay higher returns for taking higher risks. So a higher cap rate can mean a riskier property to own or a more difficult property to manage. As an example, which would be a less risky tenant: a small sole proprietor nightclub property or an office for a large successful multinational corporation? A large well-run corporation is usually considered a lower risk and should have a corresponding lower cap rate. Also an office building is usually lower risk than a nightclub and so should have a lower cap rate.

The Capitalization Rate is a term very commonly used and even "over-used" to evaluate properties. Remember this is just one number. It cannot possibly determine, by itself, a good investment from a bad one. Seasoned investors use all the tools at their disposal to evaluate a property and do not fixate on one number. Look at all the information available when evaluating an investment.

Also be aware that there are people who calculate cap rates with mistakes in them. Whether this is intentional or accidental is not really important. It is important that the cap rate is calculated properly. It is a good idea for every serious investor to run their own numbers and never rely blindly on someone else's calculations.

Gross Rent Multiplier (GRM)

The Gross Rent Multiplier (GRM) is a commonly used number that when multiplied by the annual GSI will give the value of the property.

Property Value = GRM x Annual GSI

Or the GRM can be calculated as:

GRM = Property Value / Annual GSI

A property's value can be estimated by taking the annual GSI and multiplying it by the market GRM as shown above. This is just an estimate and of course depends on many other factors. Also, determining the market GRM is not a precise science. It is usually the opinion of an experienced investor or broker. Remember also that this is using historical numbers to estimate future performance.

The GRM is can be used to compare one property to other properties in the same market, similar to the cap rate. This metric is useful to get a rough idea if a property is priced well or not, but do not rely on it by itself. The GRM is very simple to calculate but does not consider vacancy and credit losses nor expenses, so it does have limitations.

Cash-on-Cash Return

The **Cash-on-Cash Return** is the percentage return on cash invested into a given property over a given period of time, usually a year.

Cash-on-Cash Return
= Annual Cash Flow / Cash Invested

This means if an investor buys a $1,000,000 property and puts a down payment of approximately 30% or $300,000 and expects a cash flow return of $30,000/year then they will get a 10% cash on cash return ($30,000 / $300,000 = 10%).

The cash flow is typically income minus expenses and minus loan payments made[1]. Also this can be thought of as a **Return on Investment (ROI)**.

What is important to most investors is: what will be the net cash deposited into the bank account at the end of every month[2] for a given investment. The Cash-on-Cash Return should be very important to every investor because it tells them the return rate on their money invested.

Time Value of Money

The concept of the **Time Value Of Money** is: The value of a dollar today is worth more than the value of a dollar in the future. If someone receives a

---

[1] Debt payments made are also known as the **Debt Service**.
[2] and when the property is sold

payment of $100,000 today it is worth much more than a payment of $100,000 in 10 years.

Why? If paid today, they could invest that money for 10 years and it would be worth considerably more than $100,000[1]. Also, most people expect the buying power of $100,000 to be less in 10 years than today; so a $100,000 would buy less in 10 years than today. Additionally, there is some risk that the $100,000 will not actually be paid in 10 years. For all of these reasons a payment today is worth more than a payment in the future.

This is why lenders charge interest; they "give" an investor cash today for a promise to be paid back in the future. The interest charged compensates the lender for taking the payment later and of course they earn a return on their investment.

Present Value (PV) and Future Value (FV)

The **Present Value (PV)** is the value of a payment made today. It could also mean the "value today" of a payment that will be made in the future, after taking into consideration the time value of money. This takes a bit of explaining but it is worth following through this logic to get a much better understanding of the time value of money and interest.

Cash Flow

A commonly used term for any payment is a **Cash Flow**. A cash flow can be used for a payment

---

[1] If someone were to invest $100,000 for 10 years and earn only a net 5% return per year this would be worth $162,889 at the end of the 10 years. This is a big difference and clearly illustrates the power of the time value of money.

made which is a negative cash flow or for a payment received which is a positive cash flow. Another way to think of this is: Payments made (paid out) reduce the amount in a bank account so are negative cash flows, while payments received increase the amount in a bank account so are positive cash flows.

A Future Cash Flow Can Be "Discounted" to a Present Value Cash Flow

A "future payment" or future cash (Future Value, FV) flow can be **Discounted** to an equivalent value of what it is worth today after taking into consideration the time value of money. It is discounted because money paid in the future is worth less than money paid now. When a future cash flow is "discounted" back to equivalent dollars today this is known as the Present Value of a future cash flow.

A Current Cash Flow Can Earn Interest to a Future Cash Flow

The opposite is true also; a payment made today will be worth more in the future, because of the time value of money. This is like earning interest on a savings account or paying interest on a loan.

Calculating a Future Cash Flow from a Present Value (Earning Interest)

An example will clarify this quite a bit. If someone borrows $100,000 for 1 year at an interest rate of 10% (10% = 0.10) per year they will owe $100,000 x (1 + 0.10) = $110,000 at the end of the year. This is the Future Value. A simple formula to show this is:

Future Value$_{EndofYear1}$
= Current Value x (1 + Interest Rate)

Or in a commonly used shorter notation:

FV_{Yr1} = PV x (1 + i)

Where:
FV_{Yr1} is Future Value at the end of year 1
PV is Present Value (current value)
i is the interest rate per period of time

The value of future payments is called the Future Value and notated by FV. The value of a payment made now is called the Present Value and is notated by PV.

The "Period" of time is one year in this example. Now if the period of time is changed to 2 years the formula would become this amount shown above plus one more year's worth of interest charges. Or to follow the example it would be:

$110,000 x (1+0.10) = $112,000
which is the same as:
= $100,000 x (1+0.10) x (1+0.10)
= $100,000 x (1+0.10)^2

Note that the interest **Compounds** which simply means that interest is charged not only on the original amount but also on interest already accrued[1]. How often this is calculated is called the **Compounding Period**. In this example it is **Compounded Annually** or in other words once per year. In practice it is often compounded every month (**Compounded Monthly**).

---

[1] In this example we are assuming no payments are made.

So if the amount owed at the end of year 1 is taken and then interest is added on for year two just like in year 1 like the numerical example above this becomes:

$$FV_{Yr2} = FV_{Yr1} \times (1 + i)$$

and since $FV_{Yr1} = PV \times (1 + i)$

$$FV_{Yr2} = PV \times (1 + i) \times (1 + i)$$
$$\text{or}$$
$$= PV \times (1 + i)^2$$

For 3 yrs it would be:

$$FV_{Yr3} = PV \times (1 + i) \times (1 + i) \times (1 + i)$$
$$\text{or}$$
$$= PV \times (1 + i)^3$$

And so on for more and more years. This can be put into a formula to calculate a Future Value (FV) from a Present Value (PV) as:

$FV = PV \times (1 + i)^n$
Where
> **n is the number of periods of time[1]**
> **i is the interest rate per period**
> **PV the Present Value or current value**
> **FV is the Future Value**

Remember this is like earning interest on a savings account or paying interest on a loan[2].

---

[1] n is the number of periods of time, not the length of the periods of time.

[2] Assuming no payments are made. The case when payments are made will be discussed in the chapter on Financing.

Calculating Present Value from Future a Cash Flow

The formula shown above to calculate the Future Value from a present value is:

$$FV = PV \times (1 + i)^n \quad \text{(calculate FV from PV)}$$

The opposite can also be done. Or in other words, it is possible to calculate the Present Value from a Future Value of a single cash flow in the future. With just a little algebra the formula above becomes:

$$PV = FV / (1 + i)^n \quad \textbf{(calculate PV from FV)}$$

This is a way to "discount" a future cash flow back to a present value. For this reason "i" is often called a **Discount Rate**.

For example if an investor expects a $100,000 to be received in 5 years with a 6% annual discount rate compounded monthly[1]:

---

[1] Be careful to make the compounding period match the interest rate / compounding period and n the number of compounding periods. In other words: If the compounding period is monthly then i = %/mo and n is in months. If the compounding period is annual then i = %/yr and n is in years.

Compounded monthly so use month as period and interest rate in %/month

5yrs x 12months/yr = 60months

6%/year x 1yr/12months = 0.5%/month
= 0.005/month

PV = $100,000 / (1 + 0.005)^{60} = $74,137

This means that a $100,000 dollars to be paid in 5yrs is worth only $74,137 today under the given conditions.

Note that the notation $(1 + 0.005)^{60}$ means multiply 1.005 by itself 60 times[1]. Mathematicians call this a "power" or x^y means "x is raised to the power of y". This is a common function on financial calculators.

Calculating PV is the Opposite of Calculating FV

It is interesting to note that calculating FV's is just the inverse (or opposite) of calculating PV's. If you convert a PV to an FV and then back to a PV you will get the same number; as expected. From the above examples, a PV of $100,000 becomes a FV of $134,885 in 5yrs by putting it in a savings account for 5yrs at 6%/yr interest. Now if this same amount ($134,885) is discounted back from a FV to a PV using the 2nd formula the PV is $100,000.

This makes sense because the PV should equal the PV, of course. And getting $100,000 today is the same as getting $134,885 in 5yrs from now. This is the concept of the **Time Value Of Money**.

---

[1] For example, 5^2 = 5 x 5 and 5^3 = 5 x 5 x 5 and 5^4 = 5 x 5 x 5 x 5 and so on

Avoiding Errors in FV and PV Calculations

Remember for percentages,

$0.5\% = 0.5/100 = 5/1000 = 0.005$

$1\% = 1/100 = 0.01$

$5\% = 5/100 = 0.05$

$10\% = 10/100 = 0.10$

and so on in calculations

A crucial detail to understand that will help avoid major calculation errors is: Use the correct **Compounding Period**. The interest rate (i) must be in % per **Compounding Period** and the number of periods (n) needs to be the number of compounding periods in the loan term. This period can be any length of time; however, months are commonly used and sometimes years or other units are used.

For example, assume there is a loan that has a 10% / year interest rate and is for 5yrs. However, if the loan is compounded **monthly**, then $n \neq 5$ and $i \neq 10\%$ because interest is compounded monthly not annually. The number of periods needs to be converted to months and the interest rate needs to be converted to % / month to match the compounding period. Fortunately, this is easy. 5 years is the same as 5 yrs x 12 months/yr = 60 months. And 10% per year is 10% / 12 months ≈ 0.8333% / month. More generally,

- Multiply the number of yrs by 12 to convert yrs to months

- Divide the annual interest rate by 12 to convert from %/yr to %/month[1]

Lastly, the interest rate must agree in units with the number of periods in the term of the loan. If the compounding period was already considered, then this is already taken care of. To avoid calculation errors make sure if the interest rate is in % per month then the number of periods is also in months. And if it is in % per year then the number of periods needs to also be in years. They need to match. For example, 5yrs and 12%/yr compounded annually; or alternatively 60 months and 0.5%/month compounded monthly.

Here is an example for $100,000 put into a savings account for 5 years with a 6% annual interest rate compounded monthly:

Compounded monthly so use month as period and interest rate in %/month

5yrs x 12months/yr = 60months

6%/yr x 1yr/12months=0.5%/month=0.005/month

$FV = \$100,000 \times (1 + 0.005)^{60} = \$134,885$

Using a Financial Calculator to Calculate Present Value from a Single Future Cash Flow

To Calculate a Present Value (PV) from one future cash flow, enter the following into a financial calculator:

---

[1] Most financial calculators will do these year-to-month conversions if the correct buttons are pushed. See your calculator's manual for more details.

Robert's Guide to Commercial Real Estate Investments

- **n is the number of periods (be sure this in the same units like months or years as the compounding period)**
- **i is the interest rate per period (be sure this is in the same units also, like %/month or %/year)**
- **FV is the amount to be paid in the future. This is the future cash flow.**
- **PMT is 0 because there are no other cash flows so no payments are made** (to be explained in more detail in the section on financing and loans)
- **Solve for the Present Value (PV)[1]**

Using a Financial Calculator to Calculate the Future Value from the Present Value

To Calculate a Future Value (FV) from a current cash flow paid today, enter the following into a financial calculator:

- **n is the number of periods (be sure this in the same units like months or years as the compounding period)**
- **i is the interest rate per period (be sure this is in the same units also, like %/month or %/year)**
- **PV is the amount paid today. This is the present value like an amount deposited into a interest earning/bearing savings account.**
- **PMT is 0 because there are no other cash flows so no payments are made** (to be

---

[1] Usually done by pressing the key marked as PV

explained in more detail in the section on financing and loans)
- **Solve for the Future Value (FV)**[1]

Investors Trade a Current Negative Cash Flow for an Expectation of a Future Positive Cash Flows

All of this is extremely valuable, because all investments are based on the assumption if an investor buys something today (negative current cash flow, PV) that they will receive net income in the future (future positive cash flows, FV's)[2].

After all. doesn't every property owner spend money to buy real estate that they expect to pay future cash flows? The key question is: "What are these future cash flows worth **today?**" or in other words "How much should be paid for a property **today?**". The answer to this question is the **Net Present Value**.

Net Present Value (NPV)

The **Net Present Value (NPV)** is simply the sum of all expected current and future cash flows (positive and negative, income and expenses and initial costs) converted to Present Values (PV) and then added up to show the total present value or **Net Present Value**. This gives investors another method to compare properties.

---

[1] Usually done by pressing the key marked as FV

[2] They will also incur expenses, which are future negative cash flows (FV's), but the income should more than offset the expenses so there is positive "Net Income". Net is income less expenses.

Here is the idea. The investor picks a period of time that they would plan to hold a property. This is commonly called a **Holding Period**. 3, 5, 7, or 10 years are common, but certainly not the only possibilities. During this holding period there are a number of expected future cash flows due to income and expenses. The investor converts each of these predicted future cash flows (FV) to Present Values (PV) using the formula above or a financial calculator and then simply adds them up to a Net Present Value (NPV).

When doing this the investor must take care with ± sign of the cash flows:

- Negative for cash "outflows" from the investor
- Positive for cash "inflows" to the investor

These future cash flows should include:

- All expected income (positive cash flow)
- Expenses (negative cash flow)
- Loan payments[1] (negative cash flow)
- Cash invested to purchase the property (negative cash flow) including buyer costs to purchase
- Net sales proceeds (positive cash flow), net of cost of sale to seller net of commissions and fees

---

[1] Loan payments are commonly called "debt service". Calculating these will be discussed in the chapter on financing.

Calculating NPV

This gets tedious very quickly so a good way to keep track of all these cash flows is to create a table like this on a piece of paper or in a spreadsheet:

Period (j)	Cash Flows (CF_j)	PV_j
0	CF_0	$PV = CF_0$
1	CF_1	PV_1
2	CF_2	PV_2
3	CF_3	PV_3
.	.	.
.	.	.
.	.	.
n	CF_n	PV_n
		NPV total

- where CF_j is the net cash flows for each period of time j. Each CF_j is the income less the expenses for that one period.
- PV_j is the present value of that period's cash flow
- n is again the total number of periods

Now each one of these Cash flows can be converted back to a Present Value (PV_j) and then added up to get the total of the present values or the **Net Present Value (NPV).**

It is important to remember that:

- The initial time period is "0" which is now or the initial time. Period 0 includes the negative cash flow spent to purchase the property

- The last time period is n and includes the positive cash flow from the sale proceeds of the property
- Time periods 1 through n include the positive cash flow income and negative cash flow expenses

Cash Flow Notation (CF$_j$)

As shown above, a common notation is CF$_j$, which means a Cash Flow in period "j". This is good to know because many financial calculators use this notation. Each CF$_j$ can be a positive or negative cash flow.

NPV Calculations on a Financial Calculator[1]

Additionally, many financial calculators can calculate NPV directly. To do this first enter each CF$_j$ and then use the calculator to find the NPV. After entering the CF$_j$'s the NPV is often calculated by pressing the key marked NPV.

Interpreting NPV's

Higher NPV's, typically mean better investments. Also, the NPV is the estimated present value of the property to the investor and so is a good estimate of value to the investor.

If the NPV could be calculated exactly it would be easy to value a property, but remember that it is based on:

- Estimating future cash flows

---

[1] Take care to not confuse the CF$_j$ and NPV calculator function with the PV, FV, i, n, and PMT function. The first is for **Unequal Cash Flows** and the latter is for **Equal Cash Flows**. This will be discussed further in the chapter on financing.

- Estimating a discount rate for a particular investor[1]
- Choosing a arbitrary holding period

and so remember NPV is an estimate itself; a reasonable estimate, but still an estimate.

If comparing properties with different holding periods the NPV becomes is problematic, because it is difficult to compare properties with different planned holding periods. It is not fair to compare a property that will be held for 5 years to one that will be held for 10 years with this method, so be careful with NPV comparisons.

Discount Rate and Opportunity Cost

A great question to ask now is: If an investor expects future cash flows then what interest rate (i) should they use in these present value calculations. The higher the rate, the more "future payments" will be "discounted" to show their current value (PV). The interest rate, i, used to "discount" Future Values (FV) back to Present Values (PV) is normally called the **Discount Rate**. The value any investor should use for the discount rate (i) is the best alternative investment they have available to earn money. This could be the rate of return they could earn on stocks, bonds, other real estate, or even a savings account. Whatever they could reasonably achieve elsewhere. This is their the **Opportunity Cost**. Opportunity Cost is the cost attributed to giving up the opportunity to

---

[1] This may be different for different investors who have different alternative investments. Because of this they have different opportunity costs and so different discount rates.

invest their money elsewhere. So the Discount Rate is often thought of as an investor's Opportunity Cost.

Internal Rate of Return (IRR)

The **Internal Rate of Return (IRR)** is yet another metric to help investors compare properties. The IRR is the percentage rate earned on the invested dollars per period (usually per year) over the holding period. It is essentially the **Yield**.

To calculate the IRR the investor predicts all future cash flows over the entire holding period just like when calculating the NPV. However, after the future cash flows are determined the value of "i" that makes the NPV = 0 is the IRR. This is because when the PV of the investment (negative cash flow) equals the PV of all the future cash inflows and outflows (net positive cash flows) then the NPV is 0; and "i" is the Yield or IRR. Another way to show this is:

$NPV = PV_{0AllPurchaseCosts} + PV_{AllFutureCashFlows}$

PV_0 = all purchase costs, should be negative

$PV_{AllFutureCashFlows}$ should be positive

so if,

i is adjusted so that $PV_0 = - PV_{AllFutureCashFlows}$

Then[1],

$NPV = PV_0 + PV_{AllFutureCashFlows} = 0$

The IRR is tedious to calculate by hand, but again financial calculators and spreadsheets typically have a function to calculate IRR directly. To do this

---

[1] This is like 20 - 20 = 0

manually, the analysis would require adjusting "i" by trial and error until the NPV is 0.

Calculating IRR on a Financial Calculator

Fortunately, the IRR can be calculated on a financial calculator very easily. The calculations are just like the solution for the NPV. First enter all the CF_j's into the calculator just like for NPV, but then solve for IRR. Most financial calculators have an IRR function that is often calculated by just pressing the button marked IRR.

IRR is Not the Same as Cap Rate

It is important to notice that the IRR is **NOT** the same as the Cap Rate. The Cap Rate is an estimated return for a "snapshot" of one year and does not include debt service, while the IRR is an average return for each year[1] over the entire holding period. Each of these metrics or measurements gives an investor valuable additional information about the property to help evaluate it.

Financial Calculators and Understanding

All of the calculations in this chapter are included in common financial calculators[2] but it is still a good idea to understand the meaning of the "time value of money" as explained above. **Many people do not.** Understanding this concept can help to avoid many

---

[1] Technically, this could be over any compounding period, but years are commonly used.

[2] These calculations can also be done using financial tables or interest tables, but that is a much more old-fashioned and cumbersome method.

simple mistakes and may give an investor an advantage.

Remember, a calculator does not remove the need to understand the time value of money. These calculators just make it easy to calculate "time value of money terms" like, Net Present Values (NPV), Future Values (FV), IRR, loan balances, and many other commonly used numbers. A couple of calculators that are frequently used are the Hewlett Packard 15C and 10BII. However, there are many other very good ones.

A good financial calculator will make evaluating commercial properties much, much easier. These calculators are simple to use and can help to make anyone to look like a "pro". These calculators are powerful tools and it is recommended every investor buys one and becomes familiar with its functions.

There are several places in this book that explain how to use a financial calculator to give quick answers which can be very valuable to an investor. These are calculations that any investor may want quickly and need anytime.

Financial Calculators and Notation

Financial calculators often use "PMT" which stands for **Payment**. This is the payment on a loan which has not yet been discussed, but will be included in the chapter on financing.

This book intentionally uses:

- PV for present value
- FV for future value
- n for the number of periods

- i for the interest rate per period
- PMT for a constant periodic payment (equal cash flows)[1]

for notation because this is the same notation commonly used on financial calculators. This should make using and understanding a financial calculator much easier.

Financial calculators take ANY 4 of these terms and can calculate (or solve for) the 5th unknown term. This is very powerful!

Other common notation used in this book and by many financial calculators is:

- NPV for Net Present Value
- IRR for Internal Rate of Return
- CF_j for Cash Flow in Period "j". This is for unequal cash flows.

Property Value Appreciation

Property Value Appreciation will change the sale price when a property is sold in the future. This will increase the CF_n or final positive cash flow to the investor, so it is important to understand it in the analysis.

In the short-term appreciation is difficult, if not impossible to predict. There is no widely accepted way to predict appreciation. Many investors will just assume a constant growth rate of 3% to 5% per year[2].

---

[1] PMT will be explained further in the chapter on financing.

[2] This is the same as multiplying the property value by (1 + appreciation percentage rate/yr) for each year of appreciation. Note that this is just like

Others will not count on any appreciation in their analysis. The latter is a bit more conservative. It is up to the individual investor to choose how to conduct their analysis. And the value of the property could drop, so there is not always positive appreciation.

In the short term, property values may jump up, stay level, or drop and there does not seem to be a great model for predicting this. In the long term real estate prices seem to trend upward. So a constant growth rate model may be good in the long term, but probably not in the short term.

It is usually risky to buy a property based solely on its expected appreciation, especially when appreciation in the short term is so hard to predict. Unless the investor has lots of money and so can "ride out" any short-term "rough spots" it is probably better to avoid **Appreciation Investments**". Remember, the loan payments and expenses will keep coming even if the property drops in value. Buying properties based on their income earning potential is usually more predictable and less risky.

Evaluating a Property

When evaluating a property question everything and take very little for granted. Everyone should do their own analysis. Don't rely on others' calculations. They could have mistakes and/or intentionally misleading information. There are many ways to make mistakes so verify everything possible.

– Use real, historical income and expenses.

---

earning interest so the formula is (1 + appreciation percentage rate/yr)^y where y is the number of years of appreciation.

- Use actual expected rents from a rent roll and/or lease abstract.
- Be careful of Pro Forma numbers; they can be very misleading.
- Verify the income and expenses by comparing to the last 2 or 3 years of income and expenses. If there are any upward or downward trends be sure to find out why. Is there anything unusual going on with that property or in the market?
- Are there expense or income items that should be added or should be removed?
- Are there any inconsistencies?
- Will the management fees or property taxes change substantially if the investor buys the property?
- Make sure there are no unexpected Capital Expenditures in the near future. Or at least understand the expected ones.

Always check the math for mistakes. As a "**Sanity Check**[1]" figure out a second way to get a rough estimate of any calculated metrics to see if the calculation is even reasonable. If someone comes up with a Cap Rate of 32%; it seems very unlikely and it should be seriously questioned to see if it is correct.

Remember in any analysis: **Garbage In, Garbage Out**. Use reliable, reasonable numbers in any analysis.

Be a wise real estate investor. Take advantage of all "the numbers" available and use them to find great

---

[1] A 'sanity check" is just a rough estimate of a value by an alternative calculation method to see if the calculated value is even reasonable.

investments. Compare the calculated numbers for a property under analysis[1] to similar/comparable properties and markets.

Remember, the expected **Net Cash Flow** is the bottom line for almost any investor. Look at expected income minus all expected expenses and minus loan payments (debt service) to see what will go in the bank account month after month[2].

---

[1] Subject Property

[2] Also talk to a tax advisor to understand income tax implications.

Chapter 7 - Financing Properties:
Now It Gets "Interesting"

Financing is when an investor uses "other peoples' money" to buy an investment property. They borrow money to help purchase a property they may not have been able to buy otherwise. Usually this gives the borrower more buying power than they would have on their own and access to many more investment choices.

Lenders are the other half of the equation. They will not just loan money to anyone, for anything. They have lending requirements. Lenders want to loan money for a return while minimizing their risk. They want to ensure that any money loaned will be paid back. They do this by evaluating the likelihood that the borrower and the property will be able to generate enough money to pay back the loan.

The intent of this chapter is not to explain how the lending industry works internally nor the secondary loan market, but instead how loans affect investments.

Many of the basic terms for commercial lending will be the same as in residential; however commercial and residential loans work very differently in practice. The requirements and how to qualify are the most dramatic differences. They are a very different kind of loan. Because of this, most commercial loan brokers do not work with residential loans and most residential loan brokers do not typically work on commercial loans. There are some that say they "do it all", but be careful and make sure they can actually deliver. Would anyone want brain surgery from a heart surgeon that also dabbles in brain surgery? It is very difficult to do both well. Whenever possible use specialists.

The Loan Basics

The **Purchase Price** is the amount the property is purchased for as stated in the Purchase and Sale Agreement (PSA). It is also sometimes called the **Strike Price**, because this is where the buyer and seller "strike a deal". Typically, the buyer puts cash towards the purchase price and this is called the **Down Payment**. The difference between the purchase price and the down payment is what the bank **Loans** the borrower. The initial amount of money borrowed is called the **Principal**. Often commission and fees are added onto the amount borrowed and so the principal is:

Purchase Price

– Down Payment

+ Fees & Commissions

= Principal (Loan Amount)

Lenders charge interest on their loans because they understand the time value of money and expect to earn a return on their money loaned. A loan is an investment for a lender.

Loan Term

The **Term** of the loan is length of time until the loan is paid off.

Compounding

Compounding is a term to indicate how often interest is calculated and added onto the balance owed on the loan. It is commonly monthly, but could be yearly, daily, or any other length of time.

Amortization (Amort)

Amortization is the payment of a debt in installments over an agreed-upon period of time, during which principal and interest are paid off.

Fully Amortized Loan

A **Fully Amortized Loan** is one that has **equal periodic payments**, usually monthly, such that the loan is paid-off at exactly the same time that loan term ends. Each payment includes interest and principal payments. This is where the term **Principal and Interest (P&I)** comes from.

Calculating Monthly Periodic Payments for a Fully Amortized Loan

Calculating monthly periodic payments for a fully amortized loan is tedious to do manually, but fortunately a financial calculator does this extremely easily[1]. To calculate loan payments for a fully amortized loan on a financial calculator just enter the following information:

- **PV is the loan amount**
- **n is the number of periods (be sure this in the same units like months or years as the compounding period)**
- **i is the interest rate per period (be sure this is in the same units also, like %/month or %/year)**
- **FV is 0 because the balance is 0 at the end of a fully amortized loan**
- **Solve for PMT. This is the periodic payment. These are all payments of equal size.**

Partially Amortized Loan

Many commercial loans have a **Loan Term** that is less than the **Amortization Period**[2]. This is known as a **Partially Amortized Loan**. It is actually very

---

[1] Amortization tables can also be used, but a calculator is much faster and easier.

[2] The term is always less than or equal to the amortization period. The term cannot be longer than the amortization period, because a loan would be paid off at the end of the amortization period.

simple to understand. The loan term is the length of time that the borrower has until the loan must be paid off. The amortization is the way the payments are calculated. At the end of the term the borrower pays off the loan balance with what is commonly called a **Balloon Payment**. A balloon payment is just a large lump sum payment required in the future.

As an example, a loan with a 30 year amortization and 15 year term is the same thing as a 30 year fully amortized loan, but at the end of 15 years the balance of the loan is due as a "balloon payment". So the borrower makes payments for 15 years on a loan where payments are calculated as if it were a 30 year loan. Then at the end of 15 years the borrower pays off the balance of the loan.

In reality what usually happens is the property is refinanced or sold before the term is over so the loan is paid off with another loan before the balloon payment is due. .

Partially Amortized Loan Notation

A common notation in commercial real estate financing is to put **Amortization/Term** so it looks like 15/30 for a 15 year term with a 30 year amortization. Common amortization periods are 10, 15, 20, 25, and 30 years; while terms of 15, 20, 25, and 30 years are common but others are certainly available.

Calculating Monthly Periodic Payments for a Partially Amortized Loan

Calculating monthly periodic payments for a partially amortized loan is very similar to the fully amortized case explained earlier. The periodic payments are the same as for the fully amortized loan, but there is a balloon payment due at the end of the term. Again, using a financial calculator just enter the following information:

- **PV is the loan amount**
- **n is the number of periods for amortization (be sure this in the same units like months or years as the compounding period)**
- **i is the interest rate per period (be sure this is in the same units also, like %/month or %/year)**
- **FV is 0 because the balance is 0 at the end of a fully amortized loan**
- **Solve for PMT. This is the periodic payment for a fully amortized loan and this will be the same for the partially amortized loan**
- **Up to this point this is exactly the same as the fully amortized loan shown earlier**
- **Now change n to the number of periods in the loan term (not the amortization)**
- **Since the PV, i, and PMT values are already in the calculator and n is now the number of periods for the term, there are 4 of the 5 terms in the calculator so it can solve for the 5th, FV.**
- **Solving for FV will give the balance of the loan which is due at the end of the term.**

Calculating the Loan Balance on any Amortized Loan

The loan balance for any amortized loan, at any time can be calculated in exactly the same way discussed above to calculate the balloon payment on a partially amortized loan. The only difference is when you change n, instead change it to the period in which you want to know the loan balance. This works because the calculator already has the PV (initial loan amount), PMT (payments), i (interest rate), and n (changed to time period being looked at) already stored in it. This is 4 of the 5 inputs so it can solve for the 5th which is FV. Solving for FV gives the loan balance at then end[1] of period n.

Negatively Amortized Loan

A **Negatively Amortized Loan**[2] has equal periodic payments that are less than just the interest accruing on the loan every period. This is critical to understand! The loan amount due at the end of the term will be higher than the original loan amount. The balance due at the end of the term is also called a **Balloon Payment**.

The periodic payments only partially pay for the interest accruing so the remaining interest is added onto the principal. There is no reduction in the principal owed during the term of this loan and the amount owed increases because of unpaid interest adds to the principal. A Negatively Amortized Loan is something to carefully understand before signing up for one.

---

[1] End of period calculations are usually used in practice. However, most calculators can change to the beginning of the period calculations, but this is not used often and so will not be discussed here.

[2] Sometimes called a Neg Am loan.

Why Use a Negatively Amortized Loan

Why would anyone ever use a negatively amortized loan? It can be a good investment tool for short-term problems.

For example, if an investor finds a property that has problems like poor management, high vacancies, and/or deferred maintenance that can be fixed in a reasonable time then a negative amortization loan could be useful to buy an underperforming property like this. Because of the problems it is likely that the cash flow from this property is low so the investor may not have enough money (cash flow) to make payments on or qualify for a fully amortized loan. However, the investor may be able to use a negatively amortized loan during the time they are fixing the property's problems and so make smaller payments during that time. Then they can refinance with a fully amortized loan once the cash flow from the property is high enough to pay for a fully amortized loan.

This short-term solution can be a way to get into a long-term ownership position. The bottom line is: Negative Amortization Loans can be a very useful tool to get through a period of time until property problems can be fixed and cash flow improved. It is a short-term solution and should not be a long-term solution. It increases debt while it is in place, which is ok if this is used as a "stepping stone" to get the investor to a better position in the future. As anyone might guess, this creates risk; if the investor cannot improve the property's cash flow and get out of the negative amortization loan then there is a problem of increasing debt.

Unfortunately, some people who do not really understand a negative amortization loan will use it to buy a property they cannot really afford. Eventually they will have to pay off the loan. So in the end they make interest payments during the term of the loan and eventually pay off the principal plus unpaid accrued interest. This use of a negative amortization loan should be avoided. It just does not make sense.

Financial Leverage

Leverage is the term used to describe using borrowed money to help pay for an investment property. It is like using a "lever" to buy a larger property than could be bought without the loan.

The best way to understand leverage is with a simple example. If an investor has $200,000 cash; wants to buy an income producing property; and they purchase a $200,000 property that generates a net 10% return on investment then they will earn 10% of $200,000 = $20,000/year.

However, if they used the same $200,000 instead as a down payment on a $1,000,000 property that also has a 10% net return they would need to borrow $800,000 dollars. They are buying 5 times the dollar amount of property. And now 10% return on $1,000,000 is $100,000/yr. This is great! But now they have loan payments to make. If they borrow the $800,000 at 8% interest for 30 years (compounded monthly) their payments will be $5,870/month or $70,441/year[1]. So now their income after loan payments is $100,000 − $70,441 = $29,559/year.

_____

[1] Using a financial calculator to solve for payments (PMT).

They increased their income from $20,000/year to $29,559/year. This is leverage.

Positive Leverage

The above is an example of positive leverage. This is when the cost of borrowing money is less than what is earned on the investment. In other words, the interest rate for the borrowed money is less than the return on the investment. By borrowing money the investor's income is **increased** with **positive** leverage.

Negative Leverage

Negative leverage is just the opposite. This is when the cost of borrowing money is more than what is earned on the investment. In other words, the interest rate for the borrowed money is more than the return on the investment. By borrowing money the investor's income is **decreased** with **negative** leverage.

Why Use Negative Leverage

Why would anyone ever use negative leverage? If an investor for some reason wants a particular property, maybe it is for image or prestige, they may use negative leverage just to get the property when it is available.

However, it is much more common that the investor sees a way to improve a property significantly and the only way to purchase the property is using a loan with negative leverage. After they fix the problems or improve the property then they can get a new loan with better terms and get positive leverage. In other words, negative leverage can be used in the short-term to get into a property, improve it, and refinance with better terms and positive leverage.

Neutral Leverage

Technically, there can also be Neutral Leverage when the cost of borrowing money is equal to the income earned from the investment.

More Risk with Leverage

Not much, if anything is truly for free. There are almost always tradeoffs.   More leverage typically means more risk.   With leverage there are loan payments to be made.   The risk is that something could happen to the property or the market that would make it impossible to make the loan payments. Rents could drop, vacancies could increase, or interest rates could go up. These are all risks to be considered. However, leverage must be a good tradeoff because so many investors have financing in place on their buildings.

Advantages of Leverage

The most obvious advantage of **Leverage** is that if it is positive, it increases an investor's income.   It also gives larger income tax write-offs.   Additionally, leverage gives property value appreciation on a larger dollar amount. Although a property could decrease in value in the short-term, it is unlikely that it will in the long-term. So in the long-term it is usually better to own a more expensive property with more dollars appreciating which gives a bigger dollar gain when the property is sold.

Leverage can be used to make an investment that otherwise might not be possible without financing, to keep capital available for other investments, or to allow the investor to buy more properties and spread risk across them in-case one fails (hedging). With larger dollar amounts, investors often have access to many more investments and the likelihood of finding a good investment increases because they have more options to choose from. Quite a few "high quality" investments are only available to large investors because they are so expensive.

One other thing to remember is: For the term of a fully amortized fixed-rate loan, the payments are level, however the rents will most likely increase over time. So if loan payments are level but rental income is increasing then it seems best to own more property. Leverage helps the investor do this.

Interest Only Loans (IO or I/O)

Interest only loans are very simple. Only the interest is paid every period. Then at the end of the term the balance of the loan is just the original amount borrowed. This is paid off in one lump sum.

For example, if there is a 5 year, 12%/yr interest only loan on $100,000 compounded annually; then payments of $12,000/yr are due during the 5yr term of the loan. At the end of 5 years the original principal of $100,000 is also due.

Standard Loans

There are loans that many would call a standard or normal loan. There is probably no such thing, but it is still a common term. These are "common", "basic", "normal", "standard", "plain vanilla" loans that are typically evaluated on whether the investment property is likely to generate enough income to be able to pay off the loan. This is the most common type of loan available. The interest rates are good and the drawbacks are limited. These are often called Fixed Rate, Variable Rate, and Hybrid loans.

Fixed Rate Loans

The term **Fixed Loans** or **Fixed Rate Loans** means the interest rate (i) is fixed for the term of the loan. Common fixed rate terms are 3, 5, 7, 10, 15, 20, 25, 30, and sometimes 40 years, however these terms can be anything a lender wants to offer.

Variable Rate Loans

Variable Rate or **Variable Rate Loans** have an interest rate (i) that can adjust. The loan contract will specify exactly how these adjustments will be made.

The rates will be adjusted at specific intervals. Common adjustment intervals are every month, 3 months, 6 months, or 12 months. This is known as the **Adjustment Period**. However, it can be any timeframe. It is in the loan contract.

Typically rates will adjust by tracking a public index like a **LIBOR (London Interbank Offered Rate)**, **Treasury Note Yield**, **Prime Rate**, or some other index like these. Usually, the interest rate (i) will be one of these indexes plus some offset, called a **Margin**. A common margin is around 2.5%, but it can be anything. For example, if there is a LIBOR tracked variable rate and the LIBOR rate at the adjustment time is 6% and 2.5% is the margin then the two are added to an interest rate of i = 8.5%.

Most loans will have a minimum rate they will ever adjust to called a **Base** or **Floor Rate**. They also are likely to have a **Lifetime Cap** which is the maximum interest rate they will ever adjust to. And normally there is a **Periodic Or Annual Cap** which is the maximum they will adjust in any one adjustment period or year, respectively.

Hybrid Loans

Hybrid Loans are a combination of the fixed and variable rate loans discussed above. Typically, these have a period of time that the rate is fixed and then they change to an adjustable rate loan. Many people in this industry will say a "7 year fixed loan" when they really mean a hybrid loan with a fixed term of 7 years. Even if it is not completely accurate it is commonly used. This is probably because a property is often refinanced close to the time that the interest rate starts to adjust so the time beyond the fixed rate period is not used for the loan. Be aware of this common terminology usage. And be sure to understand the actual type of loan under consideration.

Prepayment Penalties

Prepayment Penalties are often called **Prepayments** or **Prepays** in this industry. They are penalties that have to be paid to a lender if the borrower pays off the loan early. This usually happens when an investor sells a property. The new owner gets their own financing and so the old financing is paid off at the close of the sale escrow.

Prepayment Penalties can be a fixed amount, but are usually a percentage of the outstanding balance when the loan is paid off. They normally decrease in percentage the longer the loan has been in place. For example on a 5yr loan the prepayments may be 3% during the 1st year, 2% during the 2nd year, 2% during the 3rd year, and 1% during the 4th, and 0% the 5th. This is commonly notated as: 3/2/2/1.

Underwriting

Underwriting is the process of investigating a borrower and an investment property to determine if a loan will be made by the lender. This is done to reduce the lender's risk to acceptable levels by making only loans that they believe are likely to be paid back. The employee at the lender who does this is called an **Underwriter**. For most commercial loans the focus will be on the property itself and its ability to generate income. This is very important to know. To repeat; the focus is normally on the property for "standard" loans. There are other types of loans available and other ways to evaluate whether a loan will be made but these are not the norm.

Each bank has its own underwriting criteria or requirements. A few common ones are:

- LTV (Loan to Value)
- DCR (Debt Coverage Ratio)
- Amount of Deferred Maintenance
- Type of Property
- Property Use
- Quality of the Property (A, B, or C).

This list could go on to include many others. There are more details below.

Although anyone can determine values for these metrics, the only one that really counts when getting a loan is the underwriter's value because they are evaluating if the bank should loan money or not.

All of these metrics can also be used by investors to compare and evaluate investments, but their primary importance is for underwriting when getting a loan.

Loan to Value (LTV)

Loan to Value (LTV) is the ratio of the loan amount to the amount the underwriter estimates the property is worth.

LTV = Loan Amount or Principal / Property Value

This is important to understand. The significant value is what the "underwriter" believes that this value is. They can consider the opinion of the buyer, the seller, appraisers, and anyone else, but they are evaluating the LTV for the purposes of deciding to make a loan or not. It is their opinion of the property value and nobody else's that counts. Often they will use a contract sale price, but they do not have to and may not if they do not agree with the valuation.

Banks normally state maximum LTV's that they will go up to. This is NOT a guarantee they will go that high on the LTV, just that their criteria allow them to go that high. When a loan request is made, the LTV for the request is calculated and compared to the bank's maximum LTV.   The requested loan LTV cannot exceed the banks maximum LTV.

Note that if the requested loan exceeds the bank's maximum LTV then the easiest way to reduce the LTV is to reduce the loan amount.   The underwriter will rarely increase the estimated property value to decrease LTV.

Common stated maximum LTV's from lenders range from 60% to 80% for commercial properties. There are some higher and some lower depending on the lender, the borrower, and the property. Remember these are NOT residential loans and the common rules and practices are considerably different. Usually, the property is the most important factor for giving a loan, rather than the borrower themselves.

Some investor's get very focused on the lender's maximum LTV because it is easy to calculate the maximum loan amount for a purchase from this number.   However, this can be very misleading. There are often other limiting factors in the underwriting criteria that **effectively limit the maximum LTV to a value below the banks stated maximum**.   All of the criteria together are what matters, not just the LTV by itself. A common limiting factor due to other underwriting criteria is the **Debt Coverage Ratio (DCR)** as discussed below.

The maximum LTV is typically achieved when the property and the borrower are exactly what the lender likes to loan on. In other words, what is considered an ideal situation by the lender.

Debt Service

Debt Service is a commonly used term for the loan payments made on an investment. It is typically given on an annual basis, but sometimes on a monthly basis.

Debt Coverage Ratio (DCR) or Debt Service Coverage Ratio (DSCR)

The **Debt Coverage Ratio (DCR)** is also called **Debt Service Coverage Ratio (DSCR)**. They are the same. It is simply the ratio of Annual Income less expenses to Annual Debt Service:

DCR = DSCR = Income Less Expenses/ Debt Svc

or   = Annual Net Income / Annual Debt Svc

The income and expenses will follow the underwriting standards of each lender. Each bank's underwriting has its own set of standards. It may not agree with how the seller or the buyer would determine income and expenses but this is how the bank will analyze it. Remember, what counts here is the underwriter's analysis and opinion and not anybody else's. This is where a mortgage broker who is familiar with banks' underwriting standards can be instrumental in finding a loan that will work.

Often underwriters have minimum expenses for reserves, maintenance, janitorial, and many others that the seller and buyer may not agree with. However, these are the underwriter's standards and there is usually not much any investor can do to change them.

Common minimum DCR's are 1.1 to 1.3. There are lenders that fall outside of this range depending on the lender, borrower, and property.

Prior to submitting a **Loan Request** or **Loan Package** to an underwriter make sure the income and expenses are clearly reported, accurate, and in the format that the underwriter wants. It is difficult to get a "second chance" when submitting a request for a loan. Underwriters are busy and short on time. They will usually not take a too much time to sort through unclear or inaccurate loan packages. This may result in a less than optimal loan. Remember, the underwriter is protecting the lender from risk, so if they cannot understand something in the loan package they could assume some less than ideal numbers to protect the lender. This may result denying the loan, offering a higher interest rate, or offering a lower loan amount.

It is much better to get it right the first time. This is an excellent reason to work with a good commercial loan broker. A good broker will earn their commission by finding a better loan for the investor and by avoiding potentially expensive mistakes.

DCR Can Limit Effective LTV

Depending on the market, the DCR can limit the effective LTV. To show this, here is an example:

If a property is valued at $1,000,000 and has a net income of $15,000/mo; and the lender has a maximum 70% LTV and a minimum DCR of 1.2 then the maximum loan based on LTV only would be $700,000.

However, if the interest rate is 10% on a 5yr loan (compounded monthly) then the monthly payments would be about:

$14,873/mo or $178,475/yr[1]=Annual Debt Service

Since the net income is $15,000/mo x 12 = $180,000/yr then the:

DCR = $180,000 / $178,475 = 1.0085

This loan cannot be made because the property's DCR is less than the banks minimum of 1.2 (1.0085 < 1.2).

Realistically, the income and expenses cannot be changed immediately so they cannot be used to increase the property's DCR. The only practical option to increase the DCR is to reduce the debt service (loan payments). This means reducing the loan amount, reducing the interest rate, or increasing the length of the loan term. The most straightforward option is to reduce the loan amount which effectively reduces the maximum LTV. This means the DCR can reduce the "effective LTV".

Otherwise, the investor would have to try to find a different loan program that would have a lower interest rate or a longer loan term and try to meet the DCR criteria with that loan program.

A continuation of the above example should clarify how the DCR can limit the "effective LTV".

---

[1] Using a financial calculator where PV=$700,000, i=10/12%/mo, n=5x12 = 60months, and FV =0 then solving for PMT = $14,873/mo x 12 = $178,475/yr

First, find the maximum loan amount that will reach the minimum annual debt service. This will require using the following formula from above:

DCR = Annual Net Income / Annual Debt Service

with a little algebra this becomes,

Annual Debt Service = Annual Net Income / DCR

Using the same values from the example above,

Annual Debt Service = $180,000 / 1.2
                    = $150,000/yr

Then dividing by 12 to get the monthly payment,

$150,000/yr / 12 = $12,500/mo = PMT

Now back to the financial calculator to calculate PV which is the maximum loan value. From before, i = 10/12%/mo, n = 5 x 12 = 60months, and FV =0. And PMT = $12,500/mo as calculated.

Solving for FV = $588,317 gives the **maximum loan amount limited by the minimum DCR criteria**. Now calculating the LTV:

LTV = $588,317 / $1,000,000 = 58.83%

This is considerably less than the stated maximum 70% LTV. In effect the maximum LTV has been reduced by the DCR.

Many lenders have different LTV's and DCR's depending on the property type and property use. For example, land usually has low maximum LTV's of 40-65%, while multifamily usually has fairly high maximum LTV's of 70-80%. Banks have more stringent underwriting criteria for land because it is usually riskier than an income producing property, like multifamily.

Other Underwriting Criteria

Generally, the more risk a lender perceives in a property, the more stringent they make their underwriting criteria to reduce their risk to an acceptable level. They can make more stringent underwriting criteria by decreasing the maximum LTV and/or increasing the minimum DCR[1]. Sometimes, a lender may even not lend for certain types of properties. The following things often increase perceived risk to a lender:

- Deferred Maintenance
- Certain types of properties and uses like bars, adult clubs/stores, etc.
- Cash businesses like nail salons, dry cleaners, etc. because it is difficult to know real income, owners may not report all income
- Properties with environmental risks like automobile service stations or gas stations
- Properties in neighborhoods with more crime (C quality).
- And there can be many other criteria depending on the lender

Specialty Lenders and Difficult to Finance Properties

Even properties that are difficult to finance usually have a financing solution. There is usually some specialty lender who can be found for almost any kind of property. However, these specialty lenders usually

---

[1] and the higher interest and fees they charge

charge more interest and fees to compensate them for risk. A loan broker can be very helpful with finding and negotiating these types of loans.

Hard Money Loans

Hard Money Loans are loans that are typically made when a traditional lender cannot be found to make the loan. These are high-risk, short-term **Interim Loans** typically from a few months to 3yrs long. Interest rates and points are high because these are high risk loans that the lender needs to be compensated for.

Bridge Loans

Hard money loans are often made to bridge a period of time while a property is developed, rehabilitated, rebuilt, or initially built. When used like this they are commonly called **Bridge Loans**. For this type of use it is essentially a short-term **Construction Loan**.

Hard money loans can also be useful for bridging a gap in time while long-term refinancing is put in place. This is another type of **Bridge Loan** and can occur when one loan term ends before new long-term financing can be arranged.

Hard money loans can be used to quickly purchase a property that comes up for sale. Sometimes a seller needs a quick sale and does not have time to wait for a buyer with a traditional lender to close the sale. A hard money lender can usually make very quick lending decisions and help with a quick sale. Once the hard money loan is in place the borrower has time to find long-term financing.

Take-Out Loan or Permanent Loan

The long-term financing that replaces a short-term hard money loan is often called a **Take-Out Loan** because it takes out the short-term interim financing. It is also sometimes called a **Permanent Loan** or **Perm** because it is a more permanent loan solution. This terminology is commonly used for construction loans. Usually, the long-term financing has a longer term, better rate, and is a less expensive financing solution overall.

Equity Lenders

Hard money lenders are often called **Equity Lenders** because their lending decisions are primarily based on the equity of a property. Their underwriting typically involves looking at the property itself and deciding whether to give the loan or not, based on whether the property has enough equity to pay off the loan in the case that the borrower does not pay back the loan (defaults on the loan).

Hard Money Underwriting

Hard money lenders all have their own underwriting criteria like all lenders, but usually will lend up to only 30% to 65% LTV of the property value and sometimes even less. This estimate of property value is typically their own and not anyone else's. Often their value estimate is considerably lower than the owner's estimate, which can effectively make the LTV look even smaller to the owner.

They only loan up to a small LTV because if a borrower defaults and does not pay them back then they have to sell the property quickly. To sell it quickly they will have to have a quick **Liquidation Sale** to recapture the money loaned.

A Liquidation Sale is also sometimes called a **Fire Sale**. This is a term for when someone has to sell a property almost immediately and so reduces the price to a point that someone will buy it almost immediately. The property is intentionally sold at a significant discount to attract a buyer quickly.

There are other criteria these lenders have for a Hard Money Loan. One is: Does the borrower have experience in what they are trying to accomplish and have they been successful in the past. A developer that has 30yrs experience in successfully developing industrial space will have a much better chance of getting a hard money loan to develop industrial space than a recent college graduate with no experience.

Another big consideration is "The Story". Does the borrower's plan make sense to the lender? "The story" has to make sense or the loan will not be made.

And lastly and very importantly; Does the borrower have an exit strategy to pay of the hard money loan when it is due or before? If not, it is unlikely they will get the loan.

Hard Money is Not Easy Money

Some people think Hard Money is an easy loan for a hard situation. They are mistaken; that is not why they are called "hard money" loans. These are difficult loans to get and they are not called "easy money" for a reason. These are expensive, high risk loans but can be a great option in situations that have high payoffs and require fast loan funding.

Benefits to Hard Money

There are significant benefits to these loans.

If money is needed quickly these lenders can move VERY fast. Some can fund a project in a few days and almost all within a couple of weeks if necessary. One of the biggest advantages to hard money loans is very fast funding of the loan.

Additionally, they will often include an **Interest Reserve** so that no payments are required until the loan is due (or paid off). A part of the allowable loan amount is set aside or "reserved" for accrued interest. The interest is just added-on to the loan balance. This is useful while a project is being built or rehabilitated and not yet generating income.

Conduit Loans

Conduit Loans can be very attractive to investors because they traditionally have lower interest rates. However, they have some big limitations that any investor considering them should be aware of. After the loan is made it is bundled with other loans that bankers have determined to have similar risk characteristics or risk profiles and then sold off like stocks to other investors in an open market. The term used to describe loans like this is: they have been **Collateralized**.

Conduit Loan Issues

Why does the borrower care about this? Once these loans have been collateralized the borrower is not allowed to make any changes in risk to the financing. They cannot add a 2nd mortgage. They cannot prepay the loan. No changes are allowed unless they guarantee the future income that the "collateralized" loan would have generated by the loan going to the full length of its term.

The way the borrower guarantees this income is through **Defeasance** usually, or sometimes through **Yield Maintenance**. The exact method and details will be specified in the loan contract. These subjects are far beyond the scope of this book, but what is important is that defeasance and yield maintenance are expensive to the borrower. They are often so expensive that paying-off a loan is not feasible so the borrower is locked in for the full term of the loan.

There is a way the borrower can get out of the loan. If they sell their property and the new owner assumes the loan. This is often an option (depending on the loan contract) and there is normally a 1 point fee (1% of loan balance) plus attorney's fees to assume the loan. This is all great, but there is a catch or two.

If the current owner has paid down the loan significantly then the potential new owner will have to assume a smaller loan and have a larger down payment. Additionally the property value may have increased making the loan amount an even smaller percentage of the sales price. Effectively, this creates a very low LTV and high down payment for the buyer. Remember, a 2nd mortgage is not allowed by the conduit loan because it would change the risk.

To illustrate by an example; an owner purchased a $2,000,000 building 10yrs ago and now owes only $1,000,000 on it in a conduit loan. Now if the owner is selling it for $4,000,000. The buyer would have to assume a $1,000,000 loan and come up with $3,000,000[1] to buy the property. This is only a 25% LTV.

The net effect is the loan assumed can be a small percentage of the sale price which means a low LTV. This translates to low leverage and a large down payment. This is unattractive to many investors and can make a property difficult to sell.

Interest Rate Changes and Conduit Loans

Additionally, if interest rates drop then a potential buyer could get a better interest rate than assuming the conduit loan. But the conduit loan in place does not allow for this. Often, the buyer will want to be compensated for taking on a higher interest loan and ask for a price reduction.

If the opposite happens and interest rates go up then assuming the conduit loan with a lower interest rate is a great deal for the buyer. They sometimes will pay a premium for this. However, the low LTV problem may still exist.

Other Loan Types

There are many other types of Niche Loans. They may be based on:

- Business Income
- An Investor's Employment Income

---

[1] plus fees

- or An **Investors Credit Score (FICO)**, named after the creator of the credit score, Fair Isaac Credit Organization)

These loans are much less common and are difficult to make general comments about. Typically, they will have higher interest rates than a more standard loan product, but if the investor is having trouble with standard financing these may be a good solution. These should be evaluated case-by-case to see if they make sense for a given situation. A commercial real estate loan broker can help here also.

Seller Financing or Seller Carrying Paper

A seller may **Carry Paper** which means that they are lending part or all of the money to the buyer.

Always read this kind of financing contract very carefully. Make sure it is clear and contains all the details of the loan. Remember, a well written contract can help avoid future lawsuits. This contract may be more complicated than one might think. It has to list in detail:

- When are payments due?
- When are they late?
- What happens if payments are late?
- How are payments calculated?
- What is the definition of a default?
- What happens if the buyer defaults?
- What rights do the buyer and seller have?
- How is the loan paid off and title transferred?
- and many others . . .

Most investors are not experts in lending and may not know how to create a well-written lending contract that avoids potential problems and lawsuits. This may be a good place to hire a commercial real estate attorney to write the contract.

Points

Points are a fee usually paid by the borrower when taking out a loan. Points are percentage "points" or fractions of a percentage point of the loan principal. For example, 0.5%, 1%, 2% are called ½ a point, 1 point, and 2 points, respectively.

Not all loans charge points, but many will. A loan with "no points" is not always the best loan for a given situation. Sometimes a better deal can be found by paying points. An investor needs to look at the points AND the interest rate as well as all the other terms of the loan. A rule of thumb for different loans is: fewer points tend to mean higher interest rates and more points tend mean lower interest rates[1]. In other words, a payment of points now tends to reduce interest rate which reduces future monthly payments. This is a trade-off like so many other things.

Many lenders allow investors to choose a lower interest rate by paying more points when getting a loan. This is called **Buying Down** an interest rate. This means in exchange for paying "points" the lender will reduce the interest rate. This is rarely a great deal for the borrower. In many cases the decrease in payments is not enough to make up for the points paid by the borrower when the numbers are run.

---

[1] Of course, this is with all-else being the same.

On the other hand points are sometimes paid to the borrower to help with escrow closing costs. This means the lender will pay the borrower "points" but will increase the interest rate. Usually this is not a great deal for the borrower either. Typically the increase in payments is not enough to make up for the points received by the borrower.

When a lender does not charge any points this is called **Par Pricing**.

Smarter Than the Lender?

If an investor cannot find any lender for a property, then one interpretation is that it could mean lenders generally think it is a bad investment. If a large number of very intelligent bankers are saying they do not believe in an investment enough to loan money on it then maybe the investor should rethink buying it or at least rethink the purchase price.

Another interpretation is that the investor has seen or knows something about the property that the lenders do not know about or cannot fit into their underwriting model. It could be a great investment opportunity, but make sure nothing was overlooked. Ask why none of the other really smart people out there saw the opportunity, then make sure it is real and investigate it thoroughly before buying.

Chapter 8 - Contacts and Reputation:
It Is Not Just About Who You Know,
But Also What They Think of You

Some people say it is "all about who you know". Well if this is true, it is only partially true. More importantly, it is "what they think of you".

Reputation

In real estate investments, the expression that "it is a small world" out there is very true; even more than the casual observer might ever realize. Investors will "run into" the same people over and over. If someone has been treated well in the past they will remember it, but if they've been treated poorly they will probably never forget it. Wouldn't most people choose to work with people that treat them well and they like? Of course, and fortunately in this business each individual has that choice open to them.

Ideally, each investor should strive to have a reputation for being reasonable, easy to work with, and being able to "get the deal done" without wasting anyone's time. This usually will make investing more enjoyable and profitable, because it is the path of least resistance. Less time and effort is spent on battles that waste time and are not productive; and more time is spent on the making money in investments. Why would anyone choose differently?

Prisoners' Dilemma

In the science of game theory a common starting point is a concept called the "Prisoner's Dilemma". The idea is that two people are arrested after committing some crime together. Now the police have them and are questioning them separately. There are four possible outcomes:

- One is that they both deny the crime and are set free
- Another is that prisoner A admits to the crime and "rats out" his partner so he will get a lenient sentence and be released on parole. Prisoner B is admits nothing. The result is: Prisoner A walks free and Prisoner B goes to jail.
- Prisoner A & B switch their roles
- Both Prisoner A & B "rat out" each other and they both go to jail.

If both the prisoners trust each other and deny the crime they are set free[1]. This is the best overall

---

[1] I am not condoning or supporting committing a crime and lying about it. It is just a theoretical example.

outcome. It is not likely that the two middle scenarios will happen where one is trusting and one is not. If one talks the other probably will also. If there is no trust then they are likely both "rat out" the other and both go to jail. This is the worst outcome. With trust and cooperation they both get the best outcome. With distrust and no cooperation they get the worst outcome.

By this point some people are asking, "What does this have to do with Commercial Real Estate?". The concept of the Prisoners Dilemma is a simple way to show that cooperation often results in the best possible outcome; and non-cooperation can result in the worst possible outcome. This is true for most negotiations. If all parties are truly trying to find a reasonable compromise then usually there is a favorable outcome.

Reputation Building

People who get deals done, are easy to work with, and are fair are the ones people want to do business with again. These people make money on their investments and help others make money.

If someone in a negotiation is unreasonable or unfair an agreement is usually never reached and so nothing happens, except everyone involved will remember that unreasonable person for a long time. They are likely to avoid future dealings with them, which means that the unreasonable person is shut out of many possible money making deals in the future. Additionally, it is a small world and word gets out about things like this, especially if it happens repeatedly. And so a bad reputation for being unreasonable and difficult to work with can be started.

For one time, someone may be able to take advantage of the situation and close a deal; But what about next time they try to make a deal happen. The trust is gone and hard to earn back. Reputations are made this way. Taking advantage for a one-time gain can be very costly in the long-run. It can damage reputations and cause distrust in far reaching ways. Avoid this whenever possible!

Someone once said, "I tick-off enough people by accident, I'm certainly not going to do it on purpose". This is probably a good thing to remember in all commercial real estate dealings.

Reputation & Time are the two most import assets any investor has.

Do What's Right

It is better to lose a deal and keep your integrity. It will pay off in long run. Choose to do what is right. It is much more important to maintain a good reputation than make a quick dollar. A good reputation will help with finding new opportunities to make money. If ever given the choice between choosing to keep your integrity and reputation or making a quick dollar, **choose your integrity**. Another opportunity to make money is always available. However, it is very difficult to fix a damaged reputation.

Time

Everyone has a limited amount of time and it is usually not enough. Be very sensitive to wasting people's time. Someone who continually asks for information but never acts on it could be seen as a **Time-Waster**. People who "talk and talk and talk" but never say anything substantial are usually seen as time wasters. Do not be a time waster, because very soon calls and emails will not be returned; and not many deals happen with one person alone.

On the other side, do not work with people who waste your time. If the other person is perfectly happy to take time or information when they want something, but will not return phone calls or emails then they are probably just a waste of time. Do not focus much energy or time on them. There's no need to be rude to them. That would be a waste of time. Instead continue to be polite, but just stop spending time on them. Nobody knows what the future will bring and the situation could change.

Make Friends When Networking

Most everybody knows that networking is important part of this business. It may be that an investor already has more than enough contacts. However, almost everyone could use more. Work on making friends when networking. This will make it more fun but more importantly, friends form a lasting and trusted connection. A friend is a great networking contact.

When networking just try to meet people and have conversations.   If there's no connection then there's no reason to follow-up in the future and not much chance anything will happen. But, if there is a connection and a new friendship is formed then a lasting and real contact is made. This is the power of networking.

Make networking fun. Never make it a chore or other people will know it and chances of success will drop. Networking by its very nature is random. Do not make unreasonable goals like, "I have to meet 3 new business prospects tonight". It is unlikely to work, which can be seen as failure and make it a chore.

Do not "sell" yourself. People generally do not like be "sold" to and will avoid this type of "networker". Just be conversational.

Maybe make it a game if necessary for motivation. See if you can meet 3, 5, 10, or any other arbitrary number of people and have a conversation, but do not make it a chore. Keep in mind that it is like a party. Do whatever it takes to have some fun, food, and drinks while meeting fun and interesting people.

Avoid the "Card Passer"

When networking avoid being a "card passer". This is someone who runs around the room and passes out their business cards. This is such a waste of time. Nobody knows who they are or any details about them or their business. They just have a card. What is the chance anyone will remember them next week or next month or next year when they may need that person's services?

Keep an Open Mind When Networking

It is impossible to tell where a new prospect may come from. It can come from some very unpredictable places. Be polite and friendly to everyone. Keep an open mind and do not judge too quickly. Nobody can tell where their next prospect may come from. The bottom line is: Network, Network, Network. It is difficult to know too many people.

Remember to try to meet anybody working in the commercial real estate field, not just property buyers and sellers. This may be a lawyer, accountant, broker, or banker, but remember they know people also. They may have a referral or there may be a need for their services in a week, a month, or a year. These are all good people to know.

Surrounded By Great People

Successful real estate investors surround themselves with great quality people. They will know great:

- – Attorneys
- – Accountants
- – Real Estate Brokers
- – Loan Brokers And Bankers
- – Property Managers
- – etc.

Over time these people become the investor's trusted advisors. These are all people who help get the job done and help make an investor successful.

Additionally, these people may be investors and potential partners themselves. They all know others in the business and may hear about investments and buyers that nobody else knows about yet.

Having this circle of people helps an investor successfully make deals happen, because their services are absolutely needed. In addition, there is more business to be won and everybody gets more business. This positive cycle is self-reinforcing and good for the investor and their advisors.

Hiring Advisors?

Each individual has to make their own decisions on whether to hire people to help them or not. This is a big decision. It is up to the individual, but in the long-run it is likely there will be fewer mistakes and more money made with the help of advisors. Having **Trusted Advisors** like accountants, attorneys, real estate brokers, loan brokers, and property management companies working for an investor seems more than reasonable.

Yes, they cost money, but they will help avoid mistakes and in the long-run may be partners or bring commercial real estate deals to the investor in the future. They are likely to help the investor bring in more income and avoid lawsuits. It seems smarter to focus on increasing income in the long-run, rather than saving money now.

It also seems logical to hire a team of experts to increase the chances of success. Why wouldn't every investor want a team of experts on their side? These experts have a **Fiduciary** responsibility to their client, the investor.   This means that they have been entrusted and have the legal responsibility to put the investor's interests first. They are legally obligated to do what is best for their client.   Additionally, specialists tend to be very good at what they do. They will know pitfalls to avoid. They will know how to get a deal done. Having specialists who are able to get a money-making deal completed and are on the investor's side just makes good business sense.

Finding Advisors

To find good advisors, start by asking for referrals from friends and other advisors.   Shop around just enough to find ones that good at their jobs, are easy to work with, and have the right "specialization" needed. Don't continually shop around for advisors. Continual shopping usually means a good relationship will never be built up and no trust is developed. It is probably better to have an advisor as a teammate than to potentially save that additional 10% of cost.

Additionally,   most   accountants,   attorneys, brokers, and property managers are very sensitive to time.   All they have to make money is their time, reputation, and knowledge, but without time the later two are useless.   I cannot stress this enough! Brokers, accountants, and lawyers work hard and will avoid people who waste their time. Many will not even call people back they do not know or do not think are a good prospect.   This is unfortunate, because nobody knows where their next good prospect will come from. .

Take the time to find a great team of advisors. Good advisors earn every dollar and are worth it.

Remember, "**cheap can be expensive**". Be careful not to "grab the pennies and let the dollars blow away in the wind". Hire specialists to get the deal done cleanly and successfully.

Specialists

Specialists are people who focus on one area of knowledge. Their focus allows them to know the many important details in their area of expertise and to be very good at their specialty. Commercial real estate investing has many aspects to consider. It seems highly unlikely that there is someone out there who knows everything about every aspect of commercial real estate. So why not hire someone who knows a lot about one area. That is a **Specialist**.

It is much better to hire the right person for a job. For example; when looking for industrial property investments use an industrial property broker; when setting up real estate trusts find a real estate trust attorney; and so on. Specialists know their field because they are focused on their field.

Commercial Real Estate Brokers

Commercial Real Estate Brokers[1] are experts on commercial properties and help make real estate deals come together because they are experts in their fields. They usually specialize in one[2] property type

---

[1] It is common practice for all commercial real estate agents to refer to themselves as a "broker" regardless of whether they hold an agent's license or a broker's license from their state.

[2] Possibly two, like industrial and office

(office, industrial, retail, multifamily, or other specialty). And some go even further and specialize in only leasing or investments. They will know about properties, leases, and investments in their area of specialization. These are people every investor should have on their team of advisors. This is an expert that is extremely valuable.

Investment Opportunities

Commercial brokers are likely to know other investors and about other investment opportunities. This is important because: **There is no single Multiple Listing Service (MLS) for commercial properties!** There is NO single list that shows all properties listed for sale. This is NOT residential real estate. There are various online services that list properties, but often properties are included only if the listing broker requests it or if the online company "hears" about it somehow. Usually online listing information is missing quite a few properties that are for sale. And often the listing information is old or inaccurate.

Broker Networks

"For Sale" Listings are advertised between brokers via email or word-of-mouth. This network of brokers has access to many listings that are not always openly distributed. This is another of many reasons to have commercial brokers on an investor's list of trusted advisors.

Commercial Loan Brokers

Commercial Loan Brokers are experts in the area of commercial real estate financing. Their job is to find a loan for the investor that works well in the specific set of circumstances. This is very specialized work and a good loan broker is worth the cost.

More Loan Choices

Loan brokers typically work with a large number of lenders. Because of this, they can help an investor choose from MANY different loan options and from many different lenders. More options to choose from, increases the chances that a better loan and better terms will be found. An investor can also work directly with a lender without a loan broker, but then they are working with only one lender. They may save money on the loan broker's commission but they probably will not see all of the options available and it is likely to end up costing them more in the long run.

Find a Better Loan

A good loan broker, like other trusted advisors, can help to avoid costly mistakes and find a better loan because they are an expert. They help the investor sort through the many complex loan choices. Additionally they know how different lenders underwrite loans and so increase the chances of finding a good loan and better loan terms (interest rate, fixed period, prepayments, etc.). Knowing lenders' underwriting standards and formats helps the loan broker submit a well-prepared **Loan Package** which improves the likelihood of getting a better loan.

Commercial vs. Residential

Remember, residential loans are very different from commercial. They are underwritten completely differently. It is probably not the best idea to use a residential loan broker who also does commercial loans. The same analogy used before applies here: Not many people would go to a heart surgeon who dabbles in brain surgery to remove a brain tumor. Always use specialists when possible. This is not the time for mistakes. And remember, "cheap can be expensive".

Broker Specialists

Find real estate brokers and loan brokers that specialize in **Commercial** properties and start to develop working relationships with them just as with other trusted advisors. They will know about properties, leases, and investments in their area of specialization. These are extremely valuable experts that every investor should have on their team of advisors.

Brokerage Fees

To earn a living, commercial real estate brokers charge a commission that is normally based on the sale price of a building. However, this is only paid if the sale closes[1]. The commission is usually paid by the seller but can be paid by the buyer or a combination of the seller and buyer. It is whatever has been negotiated. If there is a buyer's agent and a seller's agent they will often split the commission. Typical commissions are between 2-3% for each agent. Sometimes this is lower or higher depending on the seller, the buyer, the agents involved, and the transaction. Large sales transactions of over about

---

[1] In almost all cases

$10 million often have a smaller percentage commission.

Commissions are often charged by commercial loan brokers also. These are usually based on a percentage of the loan. It is commonly 1% and is paid only if the loan is successfully funded. In other words, the commission is paid only if the broker is successful. This is how the broker earns a living.

All these commissions may seem expensive, but what is the cost of a lawsuit if something is missed or done incorrectly. Or what if the investor pays just 10% over market for a property or a seller sells for just 10% under market? Or property values or rents are rapidly dropping in the area? Or the investor does not know about the 15% market vacancy rate? Or the interest rate is 1% higher that it could have been? Or the buyer does not know about the prepayment penalties or defeasance on a loan?

Include these fees in the investment analysis. If a buying a property does not have enough room to pay for advisors, the investor may want to question if it is really a good investment.

Commercial specialty brokers can help avoid costly mistakes like these and many others because they work full-time in their area of expertise. They have education, experience, and knowledge to help the investor work though a complicated transaction.

Other Opportunities

Brokers may also advise an investor about great opportunities that they might otherwise never hear about until it was too late and someone else took it.

Negotiation Buffer

Your advisors can also be invaluable as a buffer in negotiations when a negotiation gets heated. It sounds ridiculous, but sometimes parties in a negotiation may take things personally and can make some fairly offensive comments. Sometimes peoples' initial reaction is an overreaction. The advisor can remind them this is just business and it is nothing personal. The advisor has a little "distance" and is "just the messenger", so they can gently remind the person they are talking to that there's no reason to get upset or take offense. The advisor can focus on the business side. Often this can reduce the tension and help get a deal completed.

The advisor can speak for the investor and help avoid personal conflicts. They help keep focus and perspective.

Work with People You Like

Work with people you like. There's no added benefit for an investor to work with people they dislike. They might as well choose to work with people they get along with and focus their energy on investing instead of personality conflicts.

One time I was in a brokerage office with open cubicles. There was a broker yelling and swearing on the phone to someone. I could barely believe it. He was really going at it. I asked one of his coworkers what was going on. He said, "Oh, that's just his client. That's how they always talk to each other".

From that moment on, I knew I would never have a client like that. Remember there is no reason to work with somebody like this. A client, a broker, a banker, an attorney, or anybody can be "fired" by just not working with them any longer. This is each individual's choice to decide who they work with.

"High-Dollar, High Trust" Sale

Commercial real estate investing is a long-term game. It is not a run-in, make the money, and run-away business. It takes time and work.

When buying and selling commercial properties it is a "High-Dollar, High Trust" sale. A sale/purchase of any high-dollar item, typically takes time and more importantly trust. It is much harder to sell a multimillion dollar investment property when there is no trust.

Plan on taking the time to build up a good reputation in this business. It takes years to be well established. Eventually "deals" will find you, instead of you having to search for deals.

Be a "Goto" Person

It seems like there are always those "goto" people in every business. They seem to have contacts everywhere and know everyone. This person has people looking to them for help and people bring deals to them because they will get it done or know someone who will. Strive to be this "goto" person.

Chapter 9 - "Gotcha's":
Things to Watch Out For

There are many potential pitfalls with every investment. However, the smart investor has done their homework and understands their investments. They also have a team of trusted advisors to help them navigate through every sale/purchase and to help operate their properties.

Here is a short list of potential problems that could be missed. This is just a small subset of everything that could happen, but the idea here is to catch some of the big ones.

Time Kills All Deals

It has been said that, "Time Kills All Deals". It seems that the likelihood of closing a deal is reduced as the time it takes is increased. It is difficult to say why this is, but experience shows it to be true.

If it seems that anyone is delaying for no apparent reason, watch out for a problem. When there is a valid reason for a delay the person requesting the delay can usually explain their reasons easily and quickly. However, people who are delaying for no obvious reason usually have something else going on. They may not be serious about a transaction, they may not have the capability, or they could be hiding something else. Most serious sellers and buyers once they start a sale/purchase transaction they want to move forward as soon as is feasible. They need to do their due diligence and get financing, but typically the sooner they can work through that the better.

Unreturned Phone Calls and Emails

Anybody who consistently does not return calls or emails is just not seriously working on the deal. Of course periodically anyone can miss a phone call, voicemail message, or email; but when there is a consistent pattern, there is a problem.

When time after time, a person does not return phone calls and emails they are NOT really working with the investor. Sometimes, they just want to keep it on the "back burner" just in case; or are afraid to say they are no longer interested. These people are time wasters. Why chase them down for a response? If they had a response they probably would have already returned that call or email. Experience shows that when they are finally contacted, they frequently say they are no longer interested.

Advisors

With just a little research and requests for referrals most investors can find outstanding advisors:

- Accountants
- Attorneys
- Real Estate Brokers
- Loan Brokers
- Property Managers

However, there are some advisors out there that may be a problem for an investor. The good news is that if the investor sees this, they can just choose to work with someone else. This tends to weed out the "bad eggs" that are not good advisors. These advisors eventually change jobs or change the way they work and start to help their clients. It is difficult to make a living with dissatisfied clients.

There are a few attorneys that seem to be more interested in racking up fees than helping the investor. They can focus in on any minute contract detail and make it into a battle. Decide if these points are worth losing the deal over or not. Sometimes they are important sometimes they are not. If an attorney seems to consistently find a battle with every contract then the investor should ask if they are adding value or just cost. They can kill just about any deal by delaying it with ongoing negotiations until everybody is so frustrated they walk away. They are often called **Deal Breakers** for this reason. Find a **Deal Maker** attorney instead.

There also brokerage advisors who want to get the commission or fees on the deal but will not do the work. These individuals very often do not return phone calls and emails. They do not follow-up with information and questions to their clients. They do not keep an ongoing a dialog with the investor. There should be flow of information back and forth between the investor and trusted advisors.

Also, watch out for advisors that talk too much. Make sure they are not telling everyone about the deals they are working on. They should be fairly discrete about the details of the individual's investor's dealings. Nobody wants to loose a deal because somebody talked too much.

Fortunately, all of these problems are the exception and not the rule, but are important to be aware of.

Serious & Capable Buyer

How things are supposed to work and how they really work are not always the same thing. Look for secondary effects and results of any requests. There are investors out there that will "Tie-Up" a property" even when they are not very serious or do not have the capability to buy it. Sometimes they will tie-up many properties and then just close on the one or two they decide are best. Sometimes they really do not have the financing or down payment and are trying to figure out how to get them. There are many other possible scenarios. If a buyer is not serious and capable then the seller should not consider the offer and walk away from it.

On the other side, if an investor is making an offer on a property, they want to be sure their offer looks as serious as possible. Be ready to show a serious intent and capability. Otherwise, the offer may not even be fairly considered. All offers should be written up, signed, dated, and look as professional as possible. Check for mistakes before submitting the offer.

Again, the way it is supposed to work vs. how it may really work are often two different things. There are implications to asking for long escrow, long due diligence period, or immediate waiver of due diligence. All of these things make the other parties ask, "Why?". If there is not a logical valid reason that can easily be explained it will cause more questions and possible distrust. This is not good for a successful and easy transaction.

Increased Property Taxes

This is a common issue. When analyzing a property be sure that the numbers include the value for property taxes **after** the sale not what the current owner has been paying historically. Often the property taxes will "Step Up" or increase when a property is sold. This is especially true if the current owner has owned the property for a long time and the tax assessed value is well below the sale price.

Sometimes there are analyses that do not even include any property taxes. Be sure to include the new property taxes in all investment analysis.

Income taxes

This book does not treat income taxes, but be sure to understand the implications of buying a property. This is a great question to ask a trusted advisor/accountant.

Self Managed Properties

A Self Managed Property does NOT mean free management. There is a real cost even if the owner is managing the property themselves. They are investing their own time into managing the property. When a property is sold the new owner would have to hire a new manager or take over the property management duties. Either way this is not free. It costs money or time. If the new owner is not a self manager then they would have to hire someone and pay management fees. When analyzing a property be sure to include a reasonable management fee even if one is not given in the historical costs.

Parking

Parking can be a common source of problems. Make sure there are enough spaces at peak times and that there are not tenant parking conflicts. Conflicts can be caused by having two or more tenants whose customers tend to have peak hours at the same time. For example, a gym and a grocery store where many customers from each will go at the same time on their way home from work. There are many other scenarios that could cause conflicts. Remember contented customers tend to make contented tenants who tend to make contented landlords.

Parking can be checked by going to the property at various busy times and seeing if there are enough spots. For places with large parking lots like retail centers there is an interesting way to check if there is enough parking. Go look at where the parking spots stop having oil spots from cars parking there. That's as far as people usually park. If it doesn't go out to the edge of the lot there's probably enough parking.

Some properties will have agreements with neighboring properties to share parking which is commonly referred to as a **Reciprocal Parking Agreement**. This type of agreement may improve or worsen the parking, but it usually helps because it provides more parking and so parking peaks are effectively averaged out over a larger lot.

Phase I, II Environmental Reports

If the property has been used for any kind of petroleum or chemical storage then be aware there could be environmental contamination problems. This is common for automobile service stations and older dry cleaning plants. Even if there are no obvious issues, it is still likely that a Phase II Environmental Report should be ordered for these types of properties. This will be additional cost, but usually well worth it for the protection from environmental issues.

Large Prepayment Penalties

Be sure to understand any prepayment penalties that may have to be paid if a property is sold or needs to be refinanced early. Also, be sure to understand any defeasance and yield maintenance costs for an early loan payoff.

These costs can be substantial, so understand them before you take out a loan that includes any of these. They can have significant costs if the loan is paid off early due to a sale or refinance. Otherwise they are not much of an issue.

These are not necessarily bad. Typically, in exchange for the possible "early payoff penalties" these loans offer a better interest rate and/or fees. If the loan is unlikely to be paid-off early these can save the investor a lot of money.

Tenant-in-Common (TIC)

Just because it is a TIC investment does NOT mean the investor can skip their due diligence. The investor should always thoroughly investigate the TIC investment just like any other commercial real estate investment. Some common things to investigate are: make sure the stated value of the property is not artificially inflated for that market, make sure management fees and other fees are reasonable, understand what will be paid to the investor if the net income improves or deteriorates, research the history of the company offering the TIC, understand the an individual's options to sell their investment, and understand the exit strategy and timing for the entire TIC.

Get It Right The First Time

Avoid mistakes in LOI's, Offers/PSA's, counter offers, and Loan Packages. These are all important documents. Getting it right the first time makes the investor appear more professional and serious. It also reduces the chances for misunderstandings and problems and so increases the chance of success.

Loan packages are very important to get right the first time. This is an official request for a loan. Take it seriously. If it is sloppy it may get turned down and it can be difficult to get a second chance with a lender.

"No Fee" Loan Brokers

There are "no fee" loan brokers out there. If no fee is charged then they must be getting paid some other way or they could not make a living. Often, they are paid by the bank, which probably means a higher interest rate to the borrower[1]. Remember, the section on "Points" that talked about the option for a lender to pay a borrower a point in exchange for an increase the interest rate. This is very similar, but instead the point is going to the broker. There is no clear-cut way to know if this is happening or how much the interest is being increased by a "no fee" broker. Again, not much is for free. The fee is probably just included in the interest rate[2].

When working with a broker who is charges a 1% fee the investor knows the cost. It is simply 1%. The cost of a "no fee" broker is often unknown and often a more expensive option over time. Consider the entire loan including points, interest rate and all the other loan terms. Always look at the "big picture".

Low Interest Rate

Be wary of any loan broker who promises a low interest rate without knowing any details about the property that the loan is for and does not provide any

---

[1] With all else the same.

[2] effectively

details about the loan itself. It is likely this rate will not be reached when the loan is eventually funded. The low interest rate is often a "best case scenario". The other limitations like minimum loan amount, defeasance, prepayment penalties, or any number of other limits often have not been considered and may make the loan unobtainable or considerably more expensive.

No Such Thing as a Free Lunch

If it sounds too good to be true, it is!!! There are very few exceptions to this rule. Life is full of tradeoffs and so is investing. Almost nothing is for free. It may be included in the price, but it is rarely for free.

Many people say they are offering a great deal, but if they can't or won't explain how they're doing it I would be suspicious. If there's really money to be made it is almost always earned by taking on risk or working for it.

An investor should rely on their own analysis and question numbers that are provided. Do they make sense? Try calculating and estimating numbers in different ways. They should be somewhat in agreement. If not then find out why and make sense out of them before committing to anything.

Chapter 10 - Conclusion:
Getting Started

"Getting Started" may seem like an odd way to end a book, but this book is just the starting point. It has covered the basics of commercial real estate investing. It should have given enough information to get started and be able to ask the next round of questions to start investing.

Finding an Investment

How do investor's find deals? This is a great question. There is no standard answer. There is no easy answer. A tip on a property can come from anywhere. Typically it takes a lot of hard work to gain experience, knowledge, and contacts. It all takes time and effort.

Once an investor has experience their advisors and business contacts are likely to tell them about properties that may be a good investment. However, prior to that it is a lot of work. Investigate properties that are for sale and see if there is a way to make the deal work. These can be found in the newspaper, online at commercial real estate websites, www.craigslist.com, signs at properties, commercial real estate investing clubs, and through real estate brokers. Unfortunately, many of these sources do not have the "prime" deals because they have been picked over before reaching this level. But that does not mean it cannot happen and it is a good place to start networking.

Look for properties that are not being run well. This could be a sign that an investor is not all that interested in running the property. Contact property owners and find out if they have an interest in selling their property. It is not always easy to find their contact information and most of them do not want to sell. But … the only way to find out is to ask.

Make inquiries about properties and run the numbers. Make offers, but only ones that can be followed through on. Remember, do not waste anyone's time.

Is it a Good Investment?

Once the investor finds some potential investment properties it is time to collect historical income and expense information, make lease abstracts, and run the numbers. This is a lot of work, but worth it if the investment is a good one.

Good Luck and Good Investing

This is a very general purpose book, intended to give a broad overview of investing in **Commercial**

Income Producing Real Estate. This is just a starting point for investors and there is probably never a time to stop learning more. Keep asking questions.

Watch for other books on specific subjects on commercial real estate.

Appendix – Financial Calculator Notes

Equal Periodic Payments

The following notation is used with **Financial Calculators** for **Equal Periodic Payments**:

- PV for present value or current cash flows
- FV for future value or future cash flows
- n for the number of periods (must be consistent with i and must agree with compounding period)
- i for the interest rate per period (must be consistent with n and must agree with compounding period)
- PMT for a constant periodic payments (equal cash flows in each period of time)

Financial calculators can take ANY 4 of the above 5 terms and calculate (or solve for) the 5th unknown term. This is very powerful!

Calculating PV from FV Without Any Payments

Just enter n, i, PMT = 0, FV = future value amount. Then solve for PV. This the present value of a future cash flow.

Calculating FV from PV Without Any Payments

Just enter n, i, PMT = 0, PV = Present Value amount. Then solve for FV. This the future value of a present time cash flow

This means that PV can be "solved for" or FV can be "solved for" with PMT = 0 and n and i entered into calculator.

Calculating Equal Periodic Payments

To find the periodic payment for a fully amortized loan: enter n, i, PV = loan amount, FV = 0. A fully amortized loan will be paid off at the end of period n so FV = 0. Now press PMT to solve for the periodic PMT.

Calculating the Loan Balance

Calculating the loan balance for a fully amortized loan at any time is easy with a financial calculator. First calculate the equal periodic payment (PMT) for a fully amortized loan as shown in the previous paragraph. Then change/enter n to the period that the loan balance is wanted. Now press FV which will give the loan balance (FV of the loan) at the new period n.

Note i, PMT, and PV are already in the calculator and the new n that was just entered is used to calculate a new FV at period n.

Avoiding Errors with Financial Calculators

Remember for percentages,

0.5% = 0.5/100 = 5/1000 = 0.005

1% = 1/100 = 0.01

5% = 5/100 = 0.05

10% = 10/100 = 0.10

and so on in calculations

A crucial detail to understand that will help avoid major calculation errors is: Use the correct **Compounding Period**. The interest rate (i) must be in % per **Compounding Period** and the number of periods (n) needs to match that compounding period. This period can be any length of time; however, months are commonly used and sometimes years or other units are used.

For example, assume there is a loan that has a 10% / year interest rate and is for 5yrs. However, if the loan is compounded **monthly**, then n ≠ 5 and I ≠ 10% because interest is compounded monthly not annually. The number of periods needs to be converted to months and the interest rate needs to be converted to % / month to match the compounding period. Fortunately, this is easy. 5 years is the same as 5 yrs x 12 months/yr = 60 months. And 10% per year is 10% / 12 months ≈ 0.8333% / month. More generally,

- Multiply the number of yrs by 12 to convert yrs to months

- Divide the annual interest rate by 12 to convert from %/yr to %/month[1]

Lastly, the interest rate must agree in units with the number of periods in the term of the loan. If the compounding period was already considered then this is already taken care of. To avoid calculation errors make sure if the interest rate is in % per month then the number of periods is also in months. And if it is in % per year then the number of periods needs to also be in years. They need to match. For example, 5yrs and 12%/yr compounded annually; or alternatively 60 months and 0.5%/month compounded monthly.

Unequal Periodic Payments

The following notation is used with **Financial Calculators** for **Unequal Periodic Payments**.

Calculating NPV and IRR

Each cash flow is entered into the calculator as CF_j for Cash Flow in Period "j" until all cash flows are entered. This is for unequal cash flows. This automatically enters n into the calculator. Now enter i, which must be the discount rate per period. From this information the calculator can easily solve for:

- NPV for Net Present Value
- IRR for Internal Rate of Return

---

[1] Most financial calculators will do these year-to-month conversions if the correct buttons are pushed. See your calculator's manual for more details.

Equal Payments vs. Unequal Payments

Do not confuse **Equal Periodic Payments** with **Unequal Periodic Payments** on a financial calculator. These are completely separate functions on financial calculators.

Index

Printed in the United States
151912LV00002B/79/A

9 781432 719319